Clever with Cheese

HOME COOKING

© 1994 Time-Life Books B.V.
First published jointly by Time-Life Books B.V. and
Geddes & Grosset Ltd.

Material in this book was first published as part of the
series HEALTHY HOME COOKING.

ISBN 0 7054 2042 6

Printed in Italy.

Clever with Cheese

BY

THE EDITORS OF TIME-LIFE BOOKS

TIME-LIFE/GEDDES & GROSSET

Contents

Clever with Cheese

This volume brings together a wide variety of traditional and modern recipes to make the most of the great number of cheeses from around the world.

Changing production methods mean that it is now common to find mozzarellas made in Scotland and Canada and cheddars from Ireland and the USA. To get the best it undoubtedly pays to shop around and experiment. Specialist shops can offer a great variety and are always worth spending time in, especially if the staff are knowledegable and willing to offer informed advice. Supermarkets are also able to offer a wider range today due to improvements in refrigeration, although buying cheese in the area it was produced is always rewarding; for local cheeses are likely to be at their freshest and will not have been exposed to maltreatment during transportation.

To get the best from cheese it is also important to pay attention to storage. The ideal place is a cool larder or cellar where the temperature can be kept between 10° and 15°C . If it is necessary to refrigerate then cheese should be placed in the least cold part of the fridge—usually the bottom or door compartment—and wrapped in paper or aluminium foil to prevent drying out.

The Key to Better Eating

Home Cooking addresses the concerns of today's weight-conscious, health-minded cooks with recipes that take into account guidelines set by nutritionists. The secret of eating well, of course, has to do with maintaining a balance of foods in the diet. The recipes thus should be used thoughtfully, in the context of a day's eating. To make the choice easier, an analysis is given of nutrients in a single serving. The counts for calories, protein, cholesterol, total fat, saturated fat and sodium are approximate.

Interpreting the chart

The chart below gives dietary guidelines for healthy men, women and children. Recommended figures vary from country to country, but the principles are the same everywhere. Here, the average daily amounts of calories and protein are from a report by the UK Department of Health and Social Security; the maximum advisable daily intake of fat is based on guidelines given by the National Advisory Committee on Nutrition Education (NACNE); those for cholesterol and sodium are based on upper limits suggested by the World Health Organization.

The volumes in the Home Cooking series do not purport to be diet books, nor do they focus on health foods. Rather, they express a common-sense approach to cooking that uses salt, sugar, cream, butter and oil in moderation while employing other ingredients that also provide flavour and satisfaction. The portions themselves are modest in size.

The recipes make few unusual demands. Naturally they call for fresh ingredients, offering substitutes when these are unavailable. (The substitute is not calculated in the nutrient analysis, however.)

Most of the ingredients can be found in any well-stocked supermarket.

Heavy-bottomed pots and pans are recommended to guard against burning whenever a small amount of oil is used and where there is danger of the food adhering to the hot surface, but non-stick pans can be utilized as well. Both safflower oil and virgin olive oil are favoured for sautéing. Safflower oil was chosen because it is the most highly polyunsaturated vegetable fat available in supermarkets, and polyunsaturated fats reduce blood cholesterol; if unobtainable, use sunflower oil, also high in polyunsaturated fats. Virgin olive oil is used because it has a fine fruity flavour lacking in the lesser grade known as "pure". In addition, it is—like all olive oil—high in mono-unsaturated fats, which are thought not to increase blood cholesterol. When virgin olive oil is unavailable, or when its flavour is not essential to the success of the dish, 'pure' may be used.

About cooking times

To help planning, time is taken into account in the recipes. While recognizing that everyone cooks at a different speed and that stoves and ovens differ, approximate "working" and "total" times are provided. Working time stands for the minutes actively spent on preparation; total time includes unattended cooking time, as well as time devoted to marinating, steeping or soaking ingredients. Since the recipes emphasize fresh foods, they may take a bit longer to prepare than 'quick and easy' dishes that call for canned or packaged products, but the difference in flavour, and often in nutrition, should compensate for the little extra time involved.

Recommended Dietary Guidelines

Average Daily Intake				Maximum Daily Intake			
		Calories	Protein *grams*	Cholesterol *milligrams*	Total fat *grams*	Saturated fat *grams*	Sodium *milligrams*
Females	7-8	1900	47	300	80	32	2000*
	9-11	2050	51	300	77	35	2000
	12-17	2150	53	300	81	36	2000
	18-54	2150	54	300	81	36	2000
	55-74	1900	47	300	72	32	2000
Males	7-8	1980	49	300	80	33	2000
	9-11	2280	57	300	77	38	2000
	12-14	2640	66	300	99	44	2000
	15-17	2880	72	300	108	48	2000
	18-34	2900	72	300	109	48	2000
	35-64	2750	69	300	104	35	2000
	65-74	2400	60	300	91	40	2000

* *(or 5g salt)*

Cheddar and Vegetable Phyllo Roll

Serves 6 as a side dish
Working time: about 40 minutes
Total time: about 1 hour and 15 minutes
Calories 145, Protein 6g, Cholesterol 7mg, Total fat 6g,
Saturated fat 2g, Sodium 160mg

500 g/1 lb *broccoli florets*
4 tsp *safflower oil*
1 *shallot, finely chopped (about 2 tbsp)*
2 *large courgettes, grated*
6 tbsp *dry vermouth*
2 tbsp *plain flour*
12.5 cl/4 fl oz *semi-skimmed milk*
30 g/1 oz *Cheddar cheese, grated*
¹/₈ tsp *salt*
4 *sheets phyllo dough (about 45 g/1¹/₂ oz)*

Pour enough water into a saucepan to fill it 2.5 cm (1 inch) deep. Set a vegetable steamer in the pan and bring the water to the boil. Put the broccoli into the steamer, cover the pan tightly, and steam the broccoli until it is tender—about 7 minutes. When the broccoli has cooled, chop it coarsely and set it aside.

Preheat the oven to 220°C (425°F or Mark 7). Heat 2 teaspoons of the oil in a large non-stick frying pan over medium-high heat. Add the shallot and sauté it

until it is translucent—about 2 minutes. Add the courgette and cook it, stirring continuously, until it is tender— about 2 minutes more. Reduce the heat to medium, add the broccoli and vermouth to the vegetables, and cook them until the vermouth has evaporated—approximately 5 minutes.

Stir the flour into the vegetables. Add the milk and continue cooking the mixture, stirring continuously, until the liquid comes to the boil. Add the cheese and salt and set the pan aside to cool.

Place the phyllo sheets, stacked on top of each other, on a work surface. Spoon the cooled vegetable mixture lengthwise down the centre of the top sheet. Fold a long side of the stack of sheets over the filling and brush the edge lightly with some of the oil. Fold the other long side over to cover the filling.

Brush both ends with about 1 teaspoon of the remaining oil. Fold up the ends to enclose the filling. Turn the phyllo roll seam side down and set it on a baking sheet. Brush the top surface of the roll with the remaining oil. Bake the roll until the phyllo is crisp—approximately 20 minutes.

Cheese Pinwheels

Makes 8 pinwheels
Working time: about 30 minutes
Total time: about 45 minutes
Per pinwheel: Calories 210, Protein 7g, Cholesterol 2mg,
Total fat 4g, Saturated fat 1g, Sodium 270mg

225 g/7¹/₂ oz	plain flour
90 g/3 oz	wholemeal flour
3 tbsp	caster sugar
2 tsp	baking powder
¹/₂ tsp	bicarbonate of soda
¹/₈ tsp	salt
¹/₄ tsp	ground mace or ground cinnamon
¹/₄ litre/8 fl oz	plain low-fat yoghurt
2 tbsp	safflower oil
30 g/1 oz	icing sugar, sifted
2 tsp	semi-skimmed milk
Cheese and lemon filling	
125 g/4 oz	low-fat cottage cheese
2 tsp	caster sugar
1	lemon, grated rind only

To make the filling, purée the cottage cheese in a food processor until no trace of curd remains. Add the 2 teaspoons of caster sugar and the lemon rind; process the mixture until the ingredients are blended. (Al-ternatively, press the cheese through a fine sieve, add the sugar and lemon rind, and stir well.) Set aside.

Preheat the oven to 200°C (400°F or Mark 6); lightly oil a baking sheet. Combine the flours, the 3 table-spoons of caster sugar, the baking powder, bicarbo-nate of soda, salt and mace or cinnamon in a large bowl. In a smaller bowl, whisk together the yoghurt and the oil; stir this mixture into the dry ingredients with a wooden spoon. Turn the dough on to a floured surface and knead it once or twice to fully incorporate the ingredients and make a soft dough.

Divide the dough in half. Roll out one half of the dough as shown on the right and trim it into a 20 cm (8 inch) square, then cut the square into four 10 cm (4 inch) squares. Form a pinwheel, using 1 tablespoon of the cheese filling. With a spatula, transfer the pin-wheel to the baking sheet. Repeat the procedure with the remaining dough.

Bake the pinwheels until they are golden-brown— 10 to 12 minutes. Just before the pastries are done, mix the icing sugar and the milk in a small bowl. Drib-ble or brush the sugar glaze over the pinwheels as soon as they are removed from the oven. Serve the pinwheels hot.

Fresh Yoghurt Cheese

Makes about 300 g (10 oz)
Working time: about 20 minutes
Total time: about 8 hours
Per tablespoon: Calories 18, Protein 0g, Cholesterol 2mg,
Total fat 0g, Saturated fat 0g, Sodium 10mg

3/4 litre/1 1/4 pints   *plain low-fat yoghurt*

Line a large sieve with a double layer of muslin or a large, round paper coffee filter. Place the lined sieve over a deep bowl so that the yoghurt can effectively drain; spoon the yoghurt into the sieve. Cover the bowl and sieve with plastic film. Put the bowl in the refrigerator and let the yoghurt drain overnight.

Discard the whey that has collected in the bowl and transfer the yoghurt cheese to another bowl; the cheese should be very thick. Cover the bowl with plastic film and refrigerate the cheese until you are ready to use it. Yoghurt cheese will keep in the refrigerator for two weeks.

Frittata with Mozzarella Cheese

Serves 4 as a main dish
Working (and total) time: about 35 minutes
Calories 170, Protein 11g, Cholesterol 85mg, Total fat
11g, Saturated fat 4g, Sodium 320mg

1	egg, plus 2 egg whites
1/4 tsp	salt
	freshly ground black pepper
4 tbsp	low-fat ricotta cheese
1 1/2 tbsp	virgin olive oil
90 g/3 oz	mushrooms, wiped clean and sliced
2	garlic cloves, finely chopped
1 1/2 tsp	fresh thyme, or 1/2 tsp dried thyme
3	spring onions, trimmed and cut into 1 cm (1/2 inch) pieces, white and green parts separated
250 g/8 oz	courgettes, cut into batons sweet red pepper, seeded, deribbed and sliced into thin strips
1 1/2 tsp	fresh lemon juice
2 tbsp	freshly grated Parmesan cheese
60 g/2 oz	low-fat mozzarella, cut into thin strips

In a bowl, whisk together the egg, egg whites, 1/8 teaspoon of the salt, some pepper, the ricotta and 1/2 tablespoon of the oil, and set the mixture aside.

Preheat the grill. Heat the remaining tablespoon of
oil in a large, shallow non-stick fireproof casserole
over high heat. Add the mushrooms, garlic, thyme,
the white parts of the spring onions and some pepper. Cook the vegetable mixture until the mushrooms
are lightly browned—2 to 3 minutes. Add the courgettes, red pepper, the remaining 1/8 teaspoon of salt
and the lemon juice, and cook the mixture, stirring
frequently, until the vegetables are tender and all of
the liquid has evaporated—about 5 minutes.

Remove the casserole from the heat and stir the
spring onion greens and the Parmesan cheese into
the vegetable mixture. Press the vegetables into an
even layer and pour in the egg mixture. Cook the
frittata over medium heat for 1 minute. Sprinkle the
mozzarella evenly over the frittata and place the casserole under the preheated grill. Grill the frittata until
the cheese begins to brown—2 to 3 minutes. Slide
the frittata on to a warm serving plate and cut into
quarters. Serve the frittata immediately.

Griddle Cheesecakes with Cranberry Sauce

Serves 8
Working (and total) time: about 30 minutes
Calories 220, Protein 10g, Cholesterol 70mg, Total fat 2g,
Saturated fat 1g, Sodium 300mg

450 g/15 oz	*low-fat cottage cheese*
2	*eggs*
45 g/1½ oz	*caster sugar*
150 g/5 oz	*plain flour*
1 tsp	*baking powder*
1	*lemon, grated rind only*
Cranberry sauce	
100 g/3½ oz	*sugar*
1 tbsp	*corn flour*
35 cl/12 fl oz	*fresh orange juice*
200 g/7 oz	*fresh or frozen cranberries, picked over*

To make the cranberry sauce, combine the sugar and cornflour in a heavy-bottomed saucepan. Gradually pour in the orange juice, stirring continuously. Add the cranberries and bring the mixture to the boil over medium heat, stirring constantly. Reduce the heat and simmer the mixture until all the cranberries have burst —about 15 minutes. Purée the cranberry mixture in a food processor or a blender and then pass it through a sieve into a bowl. Set the sauce aside in a warm place.

Rinse out the food processor or blender and purée the cottage cheese in it. Add the eggs and blend them into the purée. Transfer the mixture to a bowl and stir in the sugar, flour and baking powder, beating just long enough to produce a smooth batter. Stir the lemon rind into the batter.

Heat a large griddle or frying pan over medium heat until a few drops of cold water dance when sprinkled on the surface. Drop a generous tablespoon of the batter on to the hot griddle or pan, and use the back of the spoon to spread the batter to a thickness of 5 mm (¼ inch). Form several more batter rounds in the same way, then cook the griddle cheesecakes until they are covered with bubbles and the undersides are golden—about 3 minutes. Flip the cheesecakes and cook them until the second sides are lightly browned—about 1 minute more. Transfer the cheesecakes to a platter and keep them warm while you cook the remaining batter.

Serve the griddle cheesecakes accompanied by the cranberry sauce.

Ricotta Muffins
with Poppy Seeds

Makes 10 muffins
Working time: about 15 minutes
Total time: about 30 minutes
Per muffin: Calories 210, Protein 7g, Cholesterol 10mg,
Total fat 7g, Saturated fat 2g, Sodium 190mg

300 g/10 oz	*plain flour*
100 g/3^1/$_2$ oz	*caster sugar*
1 tsp	*bicarbonate of soda*
^{1}/$_4$ tsp	*salt*
4 tbsp	*poppy seeds*
250 g/8 oz	*low-fat ricotta cheese*
2 tbsp	*safflower oil*
1	*lemon, grated rind only*
1 tbsp	*fresh lemon juice*
17.5 cl/6 fl oz	*semi-skimmed milk*
2	*egg whites*

Preheat the oven to 200°C (400°F or Mark 6). Lightly oil 10 cups in a muffin tin or deep bun tin.

Sift the flour, sugar, bicarbonate of soda and salt into a bowl; stir in the poppy seeds. In another bowl, combine the ricotta, oil, lemon rind and lemon juice, and then whisk in the milk. Add the ricotta mixture to the flour mixture and stir them just until they are blended; do not overmix.

Beat the egg whites until they form soft peaks. Stir half of the beaten egg whites into the ricotta batter, then fold in the remaining egg whites. Spoon the batter into the cups in the prepared tin, filling each cup no more than two-thirds full, and bake the muffins until they are lightly browned—12 to 14 minutes. Serve the muffins immediately.

Rye Griddle Cakes

Working (and total) time: about 30 minutes

Calories 155, Protein 10g, Cholesterol 80mg, Total fat 3g,
Saturated fat 1g, Sodium 315mg

2	*eggs, plus 2 egg whites*
15 cl/¹/₄ pint	*semi-skimmed milk*
2	*large spring onions, trimmed and finely chopped*
¹/₄ tsp	*salt*
	freshly ground black pepper
250 g/8 oz	*fresh dark rye breadcrumbs (made from about ¹/₂ loaf of dark rye bread)*
	Accompaniments
175 g/6 oz	*yoghurt cheese*
1 tbsp	*red lumpfish caviare*
1	*spring onion, sliced diagonally*
1	*lemon, thinly sliced (optional)*

Whisk together the eggs, egg whites, milk, finely chopped spring onions, salt and a generous grinding of pepper in a bowl. Stir in the breadcrumbs to make a smooth mixture.

Heat a large griddle or frying pan over medium heat until a few drops of water dance when sprinkled on the surface. Drop the batter 1 generous tablespoon at a time on to the griddle or pan, and use the back of the spoon to spread the batter into ovals. Cook the griddle cakes until they are covered with bubbles—1 to 3 minutes. Turn each cake and cook the second side for 1 minute more. Transfer the cakes to a platter and keep them warm while you cook the remaining batter.

Accompany each serving with a dollop of yoghurt cheese topped with some caviare and sliced spring onion; if you wish, garnish with a slice of lemon.

EDITOR'S NOTE: Plain low-fat yoghurt maybe substituted for the yoghurt cheese.

Toasted Turkey and Provolone Sandwiches with Strawberry Cranberry Jam

Serves 6 as a main dish
Working (and total) time: about 45 minutes
Calories 445, Protein 31g, Cholesterol 60mg, Total fat
12g, Saturated fat 6g, Sodium 580mg

12	*slices white sandwich bread*
2 tsp	*Dijon mustard*
350 g/12 oz	*roast turkey breast meat, sliced*
175g/6 oz	*provolone cheese, sliced*
1	*large red onion, thinly sliced*
12.5 cl/4 fl oz	*semi-skimmed milk*
1	*egg white*
1/4 tsp	*ground white pepper*

Strawberry-cranberry jam

100 g/3 1/2 oz	*fresh or frozen cranberries*
1	*orange, rind julienned, juice reserved*
1	*lemon, rind julienned, juice reserved*
100 g/3 1/2 oz	*sugar*
175 g/6 oz	*fresh strawberries, hulled and halved, or 250 g (8 oz) frozen whole strawberries, thawed and halved*

To make the jam, combine the cranberries, orange rind and juice, lemon rind and juice, and sugar in a non-reactive saucepan. Bring the mixture to the boil, reduce the heat, and simmer the fruit for 5 minutes. Add the strawberries to the saucepan, stir well, and cook the jam for an additional 5 minutes. Transfer the jam to a bowl and chill it.

Preheat the oven to 180°C (350°F or Mark 4).

Lay six of the bread slices out on a work surface and brush them with the mustard. Divide the turkey, provolone cheese and onion among these six slices. Set the remaining slices of bread on top.

In a small bowl, whisk together the milk, egg white and pepper. Brush both sides of the sandwiches with this mixture. Heat a large griddle or frying pan over medium heat until a few drops of cold water dance when sprinkled on the surface. Put the sandwiches on the griddle or in the pan and cook them until the undersides are well browned—about 5 minutes. Turn the sandwiches and cook them until the second sides are browned—2 to 3 minutes more. Serve the sandwiches immediately, accompanied by the jam.

Figs with Goat Cheese and Walnuts

Serves 8
Working (and total) time about 30 minutes
Calones 135, Protein 6g, Cholesterol 20mg, Total fat 10g,
Saturated fat 4g, Sodium 75mg

8	*ripe green or purple figs*
8	*walnuts, shelled and chopped*
175 g/6 oz	*soft goat cheese*

Herb dressing

2 tbsp	*walnut or virgin olive oil*
2 tbsp	*white wine vinegar*
4 tsp	*finely chopped parsley*
2 tsp	*finely chopped fresh thyme*
1/2 tsp	*salt*
	freshly ground black pepper

With a sharp knife, slice the tops off the figs and reserve them to be used as lids for the stuffed fruit. Hollow out the figs with a small spoon, transfer their pulp to a bowl, and mix it with the chopped walnuts. Set the mixture aside.

In a small bowl, mix together the oil and the white wine vinegar with a fork until thoroughly blended. Add the parsley, thyme, salt and some freshly ground black pepper to complete the dressing.

With the back of a fork, blend the goat cheese with the fig and walnut mixture, and spoon this filling into the figs, packing the mixture down into the hollows. Spoon the dressing over the stuffed fruit, replace the reserved tops on the figs, and serve.

Savoury Cheese Hearts

THIS IS A LOW-FAT VARIATION OF THE RICH CREAM AND CHEESE
MOULDS THAT IN FRENCH CUISINE ARE CALLED COEURS À LA CRÈME.

Serves 4

Working time about 15 minutes
Total time: about 12 hours (includes draining)
Calories 100, Protein 7g, Cholesterol 0mg, Total fat 7g,
Saturated fat 4g, Sodium 210mg

350 g/12 oz	*fromage frais*
1 tsp	*finely chopped fresh mint*
1 tsp	*finely chopped fresh lemon verbena or parsley*
1 tsp	*finely chopped fresh basil*
1 tsp	*finely grated orange rind*
¹/₂ tsp	*whole coriander seeds*
¹/₄ tsp	*salt*
1	*large egg white*
	fresh herbs, such as mint, parsley and basil, for garnish
	thin strips of orange rind for garnish

Beat the soft cheese lightly, and combine it with the chopped mint, lemon verbena or parsley, basil, orange rind, coriander seeds and salt. In a clean, dry bowl, whisk the egg white until it is fairly stiff, then fold it gently but thoroughly into the cheese mixture.

Line four perforated heart-shaped moulds with dampened squares of muslin, smoothing out wrinkles. Gently fill each mould with the cheese mixture, set the moulds over a tray or deep platter, and leave to drain for about 12 hours, or overnight, in a cool place.

Invert the hearts on to individual serving dishes and garnish them with fresh herbs and orange rind.

EDITOR'S NOTE These cheese hearts are very delicate. If they break or are damaged while being unmoulded, you can repair them by dipping a rounded knife or palette knife in water and using it to pat the cheese mixture back into shape.

Asparagus Soufflés

Serves 6

Working time: about 45 minutes

Total time: about 1 hour

Calories 75, Protein 5g, Cholesterol 20mg, Total fat 6g,
Saturated fat 3g, Sodium 30mg

350 g/12 oz	*medium asparagus, trimmed and peeled to about 2.5 cm (1 inch) below the tips*
30 g/1 oz	*unsalted butter*
30 g/1 oz	*plain flour*
125 g/4 oz	*low-fat ricotta cheese*
³/₄ tsp	*Dijon mustard*
¹/₄ tsp	*freshly grated nutmeg*
	freshly ground black pepper
4	*egg whites*

Preheat the oven to 190°C (375°F or Mark 5).

Cut off six of the asparagus tips, reserving the stalks. Bring a large saucepan of water to the boil, add the six tips and simmer until just tender—about 4 minutes. Remove the tips with a slotted spoon, refresh them under cold running water and set aside. Add the reserved stalks and remaining whole spears to the pan and simmer until very tender—about 15 minutes.

While the asparagus is cooking, butter six 12.5 cl (4 fl oz) ramekin dishes. Drain the asparagus stalks and put them in a food processor. Blend them until smooth, then rub the purée through a sieve placed over a bowl; discard the pulp left in the sieve.

Melt the butter in a saucepan. When it bubbles, add the flour and stir until the butter has been incorporated. Whisk in the asparagus purée, which will be thin. Continue whisking over low heat until the mixture is thick and bubbling. While the sauce cools, push the ricotta cheese through a nylon sieve. Add the ricotta cheese to the sauce together with the mustard, nutmeg and some pepper, and stir with a wooden spoon until smooth.

Beat the egg whites until nearly stiff and beginning to form peaks. Add a large spoonful of the whites to the asparagus purée and whisk it in to lighten the mixture, then use a metal spoon to fold in the remaining whites, cutting and folding until evenly blended. Spoon the mixture into the prepared ramekins.

Insert one reserved asparagus tip into the centre of each ramekin, making sure it just clears the surface of the soufflé mixture. Arrange the ramekins on a baking sheet and bake the soufflés until they are puffed up and just tinged golden-brown, with their centres still soft and not firmly set—15 to 20 minutes. Serve hot

Gougère with a Pepper and Tomato Filling

Serves 8

Working time: about 55 minutes

Total time: about 1 hour and 30 minutes

Calories 185, Protein 7g, Cholesterol 60mg, Total fat 10g, Saturated fat 3g, Sodium 175mg

60 g/2 oz	polyunsaturated margarine
75 g/2¹/₂ oz	plain flour
75 g/2¹/₂ oz	wholemeal flour
¹/₄ tsp	cayenne pepper
2	eggs, plus one egg white
2 tsp	Dijon mustard
60g/2 oz	Gruyère cheese, coarsely grated
1 tbsp	freshly grated Parmesan cheese

Pepper and tomato filling

1	onion, thinly sliced
1	garlic clove, crushed.
1	sweet red pepper, seeded, deribbed and cut into thin strips
1	sweet yellow pepper, seeded, deribbed and cut into thin strips
500 g/1 lb	ripe tomatoes, skinned and chopped, or 400 g (14 oz) canned tomatoes, chopped, with their juice
2 tbsp	chopped mixed fresh herbs, such as basil, parsley, thyme and oregano

Preheat the oven to 190°C (375°F or Mark 5).

Draw a circle measuring about 20 cm (8 inches) in diameter on a sheet of non-stick parchment paper and transfer it to a baking sheet.

To prepare the choux dough, put the margarine and 30 cl (¹/₂ pint) of water in a saucepan. Cook the mixture over low heat until the margarine is melted, then increase the heat and bring the liquid to the boil.

Sift the plain and wholemeal flours and the cayenne pepper on to a sheet of greaseproof paper, reserving the bran that remains in the sieve. Slide the spiced flour all at once into the saucepan and stir briskly with a wooden spoon until the dough is well combined and beginning to draw away from the sides of the pan. Remove the pan from the heat.

In a small bowl, lightly beat the eggs with the egg white and Dijon mustard. Gradually beat the egg mixture into the dough in the pan. Cool the mixture briefly, then stir in the Gruyère cheese.

Drop heaped tablespoons of the dough on to the outline of the circle on the parchment paper: keep the dollops close together. With a dampened finger, join up the pieces of dough to make a ring. Mix the Parmesan with the reserved bran and sprinkle it over the ring. Bake the gougère until it is risen, browned and just firm to the touch—40 to 45 minutes.

While the gougere bakes, prepare the filling. Put the onion, garlic, peppers and tomatoes in a heavy-bottomed sauté pan and cook, covered, over low heat until tender—20 to 25 minutes stirring occasionally. If the tomatoes release a large amount of moisture, uncover the pan for the last 5 minutes of cooking to evaporate the excess liquid. Remove the vegetables from the heat, stir in the fresh herbs, cover and keep the filling warm while you finish the gougère.

Turn off the oven and remove the gougère. With the tip of a sharp knife, pierce the sides of the ring six to eight times, and return it to the oven for 10 minutes to allow steam to escape, keeping the pastry light and airy. With the aid of a spatula, slide the gougère on to a serving platter and fill the centre of the ring with the pepper and tomato mixture. Serve immediately.

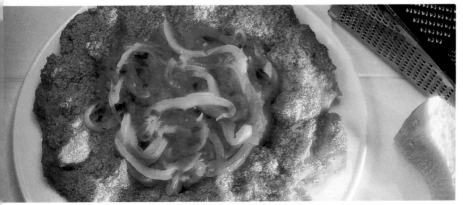

Spinach-Filled Cannelloni Gratins with Tomato Sauce

Serves 4

Working (and total) time: about 1 hour

Calories 165, Protein 10g, Cholesterol 15mg, Total fat 8g, Saturated fat 4g, Sodium 385mg

4	*cannelloni tubes (about 90 g/3 oz)*
750 g/1¹/₂ lb	*spinach leaves, washed, stemmed, blanched in boiling water for 30 seconds, drained and squeezed dry*
15 g/¹/₂ oz	*unsalted butter*
1 tbsp	*single cream*
¹/₄ tsp	*salt*
	freshly ground black pepper
¹/₂ tsp	*grated nutmeg*
15 g/¹/₂ oz	*Parmesan cheese, freshly grated*
15 g/¹/₂ oz	*dry wholemeal breadcrumbs*
1 tbsp	*finely shredded basil leaves*

Tomato sauce

¹/₂ tbsp	*virgin olive oil*
1	*small onion, very finely chopped*
1	*garlic clove, crushed*
750 g/1 ¹/₂ lb	*tomatoes, skinned, seeded and chopped, or 400 g (14 oz) canned tomatoes, drained and sieved*
2 tbsp	*finely shredded basil leaves*
¹/₄ tsp	*salt*
	freshly ground black pepper

To make the tomato sauce, heat the oil in a heavy-bottomed saucepan, add the onion, and cook over very low heat until the onion is softened but not browned. Stir in the garlic, tomatoes, basil, salt and some pepper. Cook the mixture very gently, uncovered, until the tomato sauce is thickened and reduced by half—about 30 minutes.

Meanwhile, cook the cannelloni tubes in a large pan of lightly salted boiling water until they are softened—3 to 4 minutes. Drain the tubes in a colander, rinse them under cold running water, and allow them to drain once more.

To prepare the filling, chop the spinach very finely. Heat the butter in a small frying pan, add the spinach and cook gently until it is heated through. Stir in the cream, the salt, some pepper and the grated nutmeg. Using a large spoon, fill the cannelloni tubes with the spinach mixture and place them in individual, well buttered gratin dishes.

Preheat the grill to high. Spoon the tomato sauce over the cannelloni, sprinkle them generously with the Parmesan cheese and the breadcrumbs, and cook them under the grill until they are thoroughly heated through and golden-brown—about 5 minutes. Sprinkle the gratins with the shredded basil and serve them immediately.

EDITOR'S NOTE: The cannelloni gratins may be prepared ahead of time and heated through just before serving.

Farfalle in Red Pepper Sauce with Broccoli

Serves 4
Working time: about 15 minutes
Total time: about 25 minutes

Calories 285, Protein 11g, Cholesterol 5mg, Total fat 6g,
Saturated fat 2g, Sodium 350mg

250 g/8 oz	*farfalle (or other fancy-shaped pasta)*
1 tbsp	*virgin olive oil*
1	*garlic clove, finely chopped*
2	*sweet red peppers, seeded, deribbed and coarsely chopped*
1/4 tsp	*salt*
1/4 litre/8 fl oz	*unsalted chicken stock*
75 g/2 1/2 oz	*broccoli florets, blanched for 2 minutes and refreshed under cold running water*
1 tbsp	*chopped fresh basil, or 1 tsp dried basil*
1/2 tbsp	*chopped fresh oregano, or 1/2 tsp dried oregano*
	freshly ground black pepper
4 tbsp	*freshly grated Parmesan cheese*

Heat the oil in a large, heavy frying pan over medium heat. Add the garlic and cook it for 30 seconds, stirring constantly. Add the red peppers, salt and stock. Simmer until only 6 tablespoons of liquid remain—7 to 8 minutes. Meanwhile, cook the farfalle in 3 litres (5 pints) of boiling water with 1 1/2 teaspoons of salt. Start testing the pasta after 8 minutes and cook it until it is al dente. Drain the pasta and transfer it to a bowl.

Purée the red pepper mixture in a blender or food processor. Strain it through a sieve back into the pan. Stir in the broccoli, basil, oregano, pepper and cheese. Simmer until the broccoli is heated through—2 to 3 minutes. Toss the farfalle with the sauce and serve.

Cannelloni Stuffed with Turkey, Kale and Cheese

Serves 6

Working time: about 30 minutes

Total time: about 2 hours

Calories 450, Protein 38g, Cholesterol 70mg, Total fat 12g, Saturated fat 7g, Sodium 470mg

12	cannelloni tubes (about 250 g/8 oz)
500 g/1 lb	turkey breast meat, cut into 2.5 cm (1 inch) cubes
1	small onion, finely chopped
1/2 tsp	fresh thyme, or 1/4 tsp dried thyme
4 tbsp	dry vermouth
1/2 litre/16 fl oz	unsalted chicken stock
250 g/8 oz	low-fat ricotta cheese
250 g/8 oz	low-fat cottage cheese
6 tbsp	freshly grated Parmesan cheese
250 g/8 oz	kale, cooked, thoroughly drained and finely chopped
	freshly ground black pepper
	grated nutmeg
30 g/1 oz	unsalted butter
4 tbsp	plain flour
1/2 litre/16 fl oz	skimmed milk

To begin making the stuffing, combine the turkey cubes, onion, thyme and vermouth in a bowl. Allow the cubes to marinate for at least 30 minutes.

Strain the marinade into a large, non-reactive frying pan over medium heat. Pour in the stock and bring the liquid to a simmer. Add the turkey cubes and poach them until they are no longer pink at the centre— about 4 minutes.

With a slotted spoon, transfer the cubes to a food processor, reserving their poaching liquid. Operate the machine in short bursts until the cubes are finely chopped. Add the ricotta, the cottage cheese, 4 tablespoons of the Parmesan and the kale, and mix. Season the mixture with pepper and nutmeg, and set it aside.

To prepare the sauce, melt the butter in a large saucepan over medium heat. Gradually whisk in the flour to make a paste and cook for 2 minutes. Add the reserved poaching liquid and bring the mixture to the boil, whisking constantly to prevent lumps from forming. Pour in the milk and return the liquid to the boil whisking frequently. Reduce the heat to low and let the sauce simmer gently for about 15 minutes while you prepare the cannelloni.

Add the tubes to 4 litres (7 pints) of boiling water with 2 teaspoons of salt. Start testing the pasta after 15 minutes and cook it until it is al dente. When the cannelloni are done, transfer them to a bowl of cold water.

Preheat the oven to 200°C (400°F or Mark 6). Thoroughly drain the cannelloni tubes and stuff each one carefully with the turkey mixture.

Arrange the cannelloni in a single layer in a large baking dish. Ladle the sauce over the cannelloni and sprinkle the remaining 2 tablespoons of Parmesan cheese over the top. Cover the dish with aluminium foil and bake it until the sauce bubbles and the pasta is heated through—about 30 minutes. Remove the foil from the dish and brown the cannelloni under the grill for about 5 minutes. Serve immediately.

EDITOR'S NOTE: To allow for cannelloni tubes that may tear during cooking or while being stuffed, add one or two extra tubes to the boiling water. The cannelloni may be assembled in advance and refrigerated for up to 24 hours before the sauce and Parmesan cheese are added and the dish is baked.

Ditalini Gratin with Chilli Pepper

IN THIS DISH, PASTA AND SAUCE ARE COOKED TOGETHER, WITH THE STARCH
IN THE PASTA SERVING AS THE THICKENING AGENT FOR THE SAUCE.

Serves 6 as a side dish
Working time: about 25 minutes
Total time: about 30 minutes
Calories 225, Protein 10g, Cholesterol 10mg, Total fat 4g,
Saturated fat 3g, Sodium 185mg

250 g/8 oz	*ditalini (or other small, tubular pasta)*
750 g/1¹/₂ lb	*ripe tomatoes, skinned, seeded and chopped, or 400 g (14 oz) canned whole tomatoes, drained and chopped*
1	*onion, chopped*
¹/₄ litre/8 fl oz	*semi-skimmed milk*
1	*hot green chilli pepper, seeded, deribbed and finely chopped*
1	*garlic clove, finely chopped*
¹/₄ tsp	*ground cumin*
¹/₄ tsp	*salt*
	freshly ground black pepper
60 g/2 oz	*Cheddar cheese, finely diced*

Put the tomatoes, onion and milk in a large, heavy sauté pan and bring the mixture to the boil. Add the ditalini, chilli pepper, garlic, cumin, salt and a liberal grinding of black pepper. Stir to mix thoroughly, then cover the pan and reduce the heat to medium. Simmer the mixture for 2 minutes, stirring from time to time to keep the pasta from sticking to the bottom. Preheat the grill.

Pour into the pan just enough water to cover the ditalini. Cook the pasta, removing the lid frequently to stir the mixture and keep it covered with liquid, until the pasta is just tender and a creamy sauce has formed—about 7 minutes.

Transfer the contents of the pan to a fireproof gratin dish. Sprinkle the cheese over the top and grill the pasta until the cheese is melted—2 to 3 minutes. Serve the dish immediately.

Gemelli with Sun-Dried Tomatoes, Rosemary and Thyme

Serves 8 as an appetizer
Working time: about 25 minutes
Total time: about 30 minutes
Calories 175, Protein 5g, Cholesterol 5mg, Total fat 6g,
Saturated fat 1g, Sodium 250mg

250 g/8 oz	*gemelli (or short tubular pasta)*
60 g/2 oz	*sun-dried tomatoes packed in oil, drained and thinly sliced*
4	*small leeks, trimmed, cleaned and cut into 2 cm (³/₄ inch) slices*
2	*shallots, finely chopped*
1	*fresh rosemary, or ¹/₄ tsp dried rosemary*
1¹/₂ tbsp	*fresh lemon juice*
2 tbsp	*virgin olive oil*
	freshly ground black pepper
1 tsp	*fresh thyme, or ¹/₄ tsp dried thyme*
4 tbsp	*dry white wine*
4 tbsp	*freshly grated Parmesan cheese*

Precook the gemelli in 3 litres (5 pints) of unsalted boiling water for 2 minutes—the pasta will be under-done. Drain it and put it in a large fireproof casserole. Stir in the tomatoes, ¹/₄ litre (8 fl oz) of water, 45 g (1¹/₂ oz) of the white part of the leeks, the shallots, rosemary, lemon juice, 1 tablespoon of the oil, ¹/₄ teaspoon of the salt and some pepper. Cover the casserole and cook the mixture over low heat, stirring occasionally, until all the liquid has been absorbed—about 8 minutes.

Meanwhile, in a large, heavy frying pan, heat the remaining tablespoon of oil over medium heat. Add the remaining leek slices, the remaining ¹/₄ teaspoon of salt, some pepper and the thyme. Cook the mixture for 3 minutes, stirring from time to time. Raise the heat to high and cook the mixture for 1 minute more, then pour in the wine. Cook until the liquid has evaporated—about 4 minutes.

Add the leek mixture to the casserole, then stir in the cheese. To infuse the pasta with the flavours of the herbs and sun-dried tomatoes, cover the casserole and let it stand for 5 minutes before serving it.

EDITOR'S NOTE: Two tablespoons of the oil from the sun-dried tomatoes may be substituted for the olive oil called for here.

25

Linguine with Mussels in Saffron Sauce

Serves 4

Working (and total) time: about 30 minutes

Calories 475, Protein 23g, Cholesterol 30mg, Total fat 8g, Saturated fat 2g, Sodium 560mg

350 g/12 oz	linguine (or spaghetti)
1 kg/2 lb	large mussels, scrubbed and debearded
1 tbsp	safflower oil
1	shallot, finely chopped
2 tbsp	flour
12.5 cl/4 fl oz	dry vermouth
1/8 tsp	saffron threads, steeped in 17.5 cl (6 fl oz) hot water
4 tbsp	freshly grated pecorino cheese
1/4 tsp	salt
	freshly ground black pepper
1 tbsp	cut chives

Put the mussels and 12.5 cl (4 fl oz) of water in a large pan. Cover the pan and steam the mussels over high heat until they open—about 5 minutes. Remove the mussels from the pan with a slotted spoon and set them aside. Discard any mussels that do not open.

When the mussels are cool enough to handle, remove the meat from the shells, working over the pan to catch any liquid; set the meat aside and discard the shells. Strain the liquid left in the bottom of the pan through a very fine sieve. Set the liquid aside.

Heat the safflower oil in a heavy frying pan over medium-high heat. Add the finely chopped shallot and sauté it for 30 seconds. Remove the pan from the heat. Whisk in the 2 tablespoons of flour, then the dry vermouth and the saffron liquid (whisking prevents lumps from forming). Return the frying pan to the heat and simmer the sauce over medium-low heat until it thickens—2 to 3 minutes.

Meanwhile, cook the linguine in 3 litres (5 pints) of boiling water with 1 1/2 teaspoons of salt. Start testing the pasta after 10 minutes and cook it until it is al dente.

To finish the sauce, stir in 4 tablespoons of the strained mussel-cooking liquid along with the cheese, salt, pepper, chives and mussels. Simmer the sauce for 3 to 4 minutes more to heat the mussels through.

Drain the linguine, transfer it to a bowl and toss it with the sauce. Serve immediately.

Shells Stuffed with Crab Meat and Spinach

Serves 6

Working time: about 30 minutes

Total time: about 45 minutes

Calories 220, Protein 14g, Cholesterol 50mg, Total fat 8g,
Saturated fat 2g, Sodium 365mg

12	giant pasta shells, each about 6 cm (2 ¼ inches) long
2 tbsp	safflower oil
1	large onion, chopped
⅛ tsp	salt
	freshly ground black pepper
125 g/4 oz	fresh spinach, stemmed, washed and sliced into a chiffonade
1 tbsp	chopped fresh basil or flat-leaf parsley
2 tbsp	fresh lime juice
350 g/12 oz	fresh crab meat, picked over and flaked
125 g/4 oz	low-fat ricotta

White wine sauce

12.5 cl/4 fl oz	dry white wine
1 tbsp	finely chopped shallot
⅛ tsp	salt
	freshly ground black pepper
1 tbsp	chopped fresh basil or flat-leaf parsley
1 tbsp	double cream

Preheat the oven to 180°C (350°F or Mark 4). Cook the shells in 4 litres (7 pints) of boiling water with 1 teaspoon of salt, stirring gently to prevent sticking, for 12 minutes—they will be slightly undercooked. Drain the shells and rinse them under cold running water.

While the pasta is cooking, heat 1 tablespoon of the oil in a heavy frying pan over medium heat. Add the onion, salt and pepper, and cook, stirring frequently, until the onion begins to brown—about 10 minutes. Stir in the spinach, the basil or parsley, and 1 tablespoon of the lime juice. Cook the mixture, stirring, until the spinach wilts—about 2 minutes.

Remove the pan from the heat. Add the crab meat, the ricotta, the remaining tablespoon of lime juice and some more pepper; mix lightly.

Stuff each shell with some of the crab meat mixture, gently pressing it down to round out the shell.

Put the shells in a shallow baking dish and dribble the remaining oil over them. Cover loosely with aluminium foil, shiny side down, and bake for 20 minutes.

While the shells are baking, prepare the sauce. Put the white wine, shallot, salt, pepper and 12.5 cl (4 fl oz) of water in a small saucepan. Bring the mixture to the boil, then reduce the heat to medium-low and simmer until only about 6 tablespoons of liquid remain—12 to 15 minutes. Remove the pan from the heat; add the basil or parsley, and whisk in the cream. Return the pan to the heat and cook the sauce for 2 to 3 minutes more to thicken it slightly.

Pour the sauce over the baked shells and serve.

EDITOR'S NOTE: To compensate for shells that may tear during cooking, add one or two extra shells to the boiling water.

27

Pasta Shells and Scallops

Serves 6

Working (and total) time: about 25 minutes

Calories 300, Protein 18g, Cholesterol 40mg, Total fat 9g,
Saturated fat 4g, Sodium 460mg

250 g/8 oz	*medium pasta shells*
1 tbsp	*safflower oil*
1	*small onion, finely chopped*
2 tbsp	*flour*
35 cl/12 fl oz	*unsalted chicken or fish stock*
4 tbsp	*double cream*
1/8 tsp	*grated nutmeg*
1/4 tsp	*salt*
1/4 tsp	*white pepper*
350 g/12 oz	*scallops, connective muscle at their sides removed, as necessary*
4 tbsp	*fresh breadcrumbs*
60 g/2 oz	*Parmesan cheese, freshly grated*
1/4 tsp	*paprika*
	parsley sprigs for garnish

Add the pasta shells to 3 litres (5 pints) of boiling water with 1 1/2 teaspoons of salt. Start testing the pasta after 8 minutes and cook it until it is *al dente*.

Meanwhile, to prepare the sauce, pour the oil into a shallow fireproof casserole over medium heat. Add the onion and sauté it until it turns translucent—about 3 minutes. Stir in the flour and continue to cook, stirring constantly, for 2 minutes. Remove the casserole from the heat. Slowly whisk in the stock and cream, stirring the mixture until it is smooth. Add the nutmeg, salt and pepper, and stir. Preheat the grill.

Drain the pasta and add it, along with the scallops, to the sauce. Return the casserole to the heat and bring the sauce to a simmer. Cover the casserole and simmer gently until the scallops become opaque—2 to 3 minutes.

To prepare the dish for the table, wipe any sauce from the visible inside walls of the casserole. Then top the dish with the breadcrumbs, cheese and paprika and grill it until the topping is golden—about 2 minutes. Garnish with the parsley sprigs and serve hot.

Stuffed Mushrooms with Goat Cheese and Spinach

Serves 6

Working time: about 30 minutes
Total time: about 1 hour and 15 minutes

Calories 85, Protein 3g, Cholesterol 12mg, Total fat 6g,
Saturated fat 3g, Sodium 110mg

18	*large, unblemished mushrooms, wiped clean*
6 cl/2 fl oz	*dry white wine*
45 g/1½ oz	*shallots, chopped*
1 tsp	*fresh thyme, or ¼ tsp dried thyme*
1 tbsp	*fresh lime or lemon juice*
15 g/½ oz	*unsalted butter*
¼ tsp	*salt*
1 tbsp	*virgin olive oil*
2	*garlic cloves, finely chopped*
250 g/8 oz	*spinach, stems removed, leaves washed, drained, squeezed dry and coarsely chopped*
	freshly ground black pepper
90 g/3 oz	*mild goat cheese*

Carefully pull out the mushroom stems and chop them finely, either by hand or in a blender or food processor. Set the mushroom caps aside.

Preheat the oven to 180°C (350°F or Mark 4). In a large frying pan, heat the wine, 8 cl (2 fl oz) of water, 2 tablespoons of the shallots and the thyme over medium heat. Bring the liquid to the boil and cook the mixture for about 3 minutes. Add the mushroom caps, bottoms facing up, and sprinkle them with the lime or lemon juice. Cover and cook until the mushrooms have shrunk by a third—6 to 8 minutes. Remove the pan from the heat. Take the caps out of the pan one at a time, tilting them to let any juices run back into the pan. Put them on a baking sheet, bottoms down, to drain them further.

Return the pan to the stove, and reheat the contents over medium heat. Add the chopped mushroom stems, butter and half the salt; cook, stirring frequently, until all the liquid is absorbed—6 to 8 minutes. Transfer the chopped stems to a bowl.

Wash the pan and return it to the stove. Add the oil and heat it over high heat. When the oil is hot, stir in the remaining shallots and the garlic. Immediately place the spinach on top and sprinkle with the remaining salt. Cook, stirring constantly, until all of the liquid has evaporated—about 4 minutes. Transfer the spinach mixture to the bowl containing the chopped mushroom stems, and sprinkle with pepper. Stir to combine. Break the goat cheese into small pieces directly into the bowl, then carefully fold it in.

With a teaspoon, mound the spinach-and-cheese mixture into the mushroom caps. Place them in a baking dish, and bake until they are browned on top and heated through—about 20 minutes. Serve warm.

Leeks and Cheese in Phyllo Packets

Serves 6

Working time: about 45 minutes

Total time: about 1 hour and 45 minutes

Calories 275, Protein 9g, Cholesterol 30mg, Total fat 14g,
Saturated fat 6g, Sodium 290mg

4	*medium leeks, trimmed, cleaned, sliced into 1 cm (½ inch) pieces*
1 tbsp	*safflower oil*
30 g/1 oz	*unsalted butter*
275 g/9 oz	*onion, chopped*
1	*garlic clove, finely chopped*
½ tsp	*dried thyme*
¼ tsp	*salt*
	freshly ground black pepper
2 tbsp	*single cream*
150 g/5 oz	*Gruyère or other Swiss cheese, grated*
12	*sheets phyllo pastry, each 30 cm (12 inches) square*

In a large, heavy frying pan, heat the oil and half the butter over medium heat. Add the leeks, onion, garlic, thyme, salt and pepper. Cook, stirring often, for 12 minutes. Stir in the cream and continue cooking until all the liquid is absorbed—about 3 minutes more.

Transfer the leek mixture to a bowl and let it cool slightly. Stir in the cheese and refrigerate the mixture for 30 minutes.

Preheat the oven to 180°C (350°F or Mark 4). On a clean, dry work surface, lay out two sheets of phyllo dough, one on top of the other. Mound about one sixth of the leek-cheese mixture 7.5 cm (3 inches) from the lower right corner of the dough. Fold up the dough as shown on the right, forming a compact packet. Repeat the process with the remaining filling and dough sheets to form six packets in all. Put the packets, seam sides down, on a lightly buttered baking sheet. Melt the remaining butter in a small saucepan over low heat. Brush the packets with the melted butter and bake them until they are golden—about 30 minutes. Serve them hot.

EDITOR'S NOTE: These make an excellent luncheon dish served with a green salad. Thaw frozen phyllo before using.

31

Onion and Goat Cheese Pizza

Serves 8

Working time: about 40 minutes
Total time: about 2 hours and 30 minutes
Calories 220, Protein 6g, Cholesterol 10mg, Total fat 10g,
Saturated fat 3g, Sodium 170mg

1.5 kg/3 lb	onions, thinly sliced
2 tbsp	virgin olive oil
2 tsp	fresh thyme, or 1/2 tsp dried thyme
6 cl/2 fl oz	red wine vinegar or cider vinegar
1/4 tsp	salt
1 tbsp	cornmeal
90 g/3 oz	mild goat cheese or feta cheese
60 g/2 oz	low-fat cream cheese

Thyme-flavoured pizza dough

7 g/1/4 oz	dried yeast
1/4 tsp	sugar
250 g/8 oz	strong plain flour
1/4 tsp	salt
2 tsp	fresh thyme, or 1/2 tsp dried thyme
2 tbsp	virgin olive oil

To make the dough, pour 12.5 cl (4 fl oz) lukewarm water into a small bowl and sprinkle the yeast and sugar into it. Let the mixture stand for 2 to 3 minutes, then stir it until the yeast and sugar are completely dissolved. Allow the mixture to stand in a warm place until the yeast bubbles up and the mixture has doubled in bulk—about 15 minutes.

Sift 200 g (7 oz) of the flour and the salt into a large bowl, and stir in the thyme. Make a well in the centre and pour in the yeast mixture and the oil. Mix the dough by hand; it should feel slightly sticky. If it feels too sticky, work in some, or all, of the remaining flour, if it is too dry, add a little more water. As soon as the dough is firm enough to be gathered into a ball, place it on a floured board and knead it until it is smooth and elastic—about 10 minutes.

Put the dough in a clean oiled bowl and cover it with a damp towel. Set the bowl in a warm, draught-free place until the dough has doubled in bulk—about 1 to 1 1/2 hours.

While the dough is rising, make the onion topping. Heat 1 tablespoon of the olive oil in a large, heavy-bottomed fireproof casserole over medium heat. Put the onions and thyme in the casserole and cook them, stirring and scraping the bottom frequently, until the onions are well browned—45 minutes to 1 hour. Add the vinegar and salt, and cook, stirring often, until the liquid has evaporated—about 10 minutes.

Preheat the oven to 230°C (450°F or Mark 8). Sprinkle the cornmeal on a large, heavy baking sheet. Knock down the dough, then gather it up into a ball and flatten it with your hands. Stretch out the dough by holding it at the edges with both hands and turning it until it forms a circle about 20 cm (8 inches) in diameter. Put the circle in the centre of the baking sheet and pat it out to 30 cm (12 inches) in diameter.

Distribute the onions in an even layer over the pizza dough, leaving a 1 cm (1/2 inch) border uncovered at the edge. Combine the goat or feta cheese and the cream cheese in a small bowl; dot the pizza with the cheese mixture. Bake the pizza for 10 minutes. Remove it from the oven and dribble the remaining oil over the top. Return the pizza to the oven and bake it until the bottom of the crust is browned and the cheese turns golden—4 to 6 minutes. Cut the pizza into wedges and serve at once.

EDITOR'S NOTE: To prepare the pizza dough in a food processor, put 200 g (7 oz) of the flour, the salt and thyme in the processor and mix it in two short bursts. In a separate small mixing bowl, combine the bubbling yeast mixture with the oil. While the motor is running, pour the mixture into the processor as fast as the flour will absorb it; process until a ball of dough comes away from the sides of the bowl about 1 minute. If the dough is too sticky to form a ball, work in up to 30 g (1 oz) additional flour; if too dry, add a little water. Remove the dough from the processor, place it on a floured board and knead it for 5 minutes. Set the dough aside to rise as described above.

Goat Cheese and Parsley Ravioli

Serves 4

Working (and total) time: about 1 hour and 15 minutes

Calories 430, Protein 23g, Cholesterol 75mg,
Total fat 14g, Saturated fat 2g, Sodium 490mg

175 g/6 oz	strong plain flour
1	egg
1	egg white
1 tbsp	safflower oil
175 g/6 oz	soft goat cheese
90 g/3 oz	fine fresh white breadcrumbs
100 g/3^1/$_2$ oz	parsley, finely chopped
45 g/1^1/$_2$ oz	spring onions, finely chopped
Tomato sauce	
1 tsp	virgin olive oil
1	small onion, chopped
750 g/1^1/$_2$ lb	fresh tomatoes, skinned and roughly chopped
^{1}/$_2$ tsp	salt
	freshly ground black pepper

To prepare the dough, put the flour into a mixing bowl and make a well in the centre. Add the egg, egg white and oil and stir them, using a fork or wooden spoon, gradually mixing in the flour. Transfer the dough to a lightly floured surface and knead it for a few minutes. The dough should come cleanly away from the surface. If it is too wet, add flour by the tablespoon until it is no longer sticky. If the dough is too dry and crumbly, add water by the teaspoon until it is pliable. Continue kneading the dough until it is smooth and elastic— about 10 minutes. (Alternatively, place the dough ingredients in a food processor and process them for about 30 seconds.) Wrap the dough in greaseproof paper or plastic film and let it rest for 15 minutes.

Meanwhile, make the tomato sauce. Heat the olive oil in a heavy frying pan over medium heat, then sauté the onion in the oil for about 3 minutes, until softened. Add the tomatoes, salt and some pepper. Bring the contents of the pan to the boil and cook over high heat, until the tomatoes soften—about 5 minutes. Reduce the heat and simmer, uncovered, for a further 15 minutes. Remove the pan from the heat. When the mixture has cooled a little, purée it in a blender. Sieve the purée into a clean saucepan and set it aside.

To make the ravioli filling, combine the goat cheese, breadcrumbs, 90 g (3 oz) of the chopped parsley and the spring onions in a bowl. Divide the dough into two portions. Cover one with plastic film or an inverted bowl to keep it moist. Using a rolling pin, roll out the other portion very thinly on a well-floured surface into a rectangle measuring about 75 by 15 cm (30 by 6 inches); it should be about 1 mm (^{1}/$_{16}$ inch) thick. Then, following the steps shown opposite, form it into 18 ravioli, each about 6 by 5 cm (2^1/$_2$ by 2 inches). Repeat the process with the second portion of dough.

Gently reheat the tomato sauce over low heat. Add the ravioli to 3 litres (5 pints) of boiling water with 1^1/$_2$ teaspoons of salt. Start testing the ravioli after 1 minute and cook them until they are al dente, then drain them. Serve immediately with the sauce, and sprinkled with the remaining chopped parsley.

EDITOR'S NOTE: Instead of kneading and rolling out the pasta by hand, you can use a pasta machine.

Ricotta and Courgette Tortellini with Mint-Yoghurt Sauce

Serves 6

Working and total time: about 1 hour and 40 minutes

Calories 215, Protein 11g, Cholesterol 45mg, Total fat 7g, Saturated fat 4g, Sodium 145mg

175 g/6 oz	*courgettes*
1/4 tsp	*salt*
175 g/6 oz	*strong plain flour*
1	*egg*
1	*egg white*
1 tbsp	*safflower oil*
150 g/5 oz	*low-fat ricotta cheese*
	freshly ground black pepper
	chopped mint leaves, for garnish
	Mint-yoghurt sauce
200 g/7 oz	*low-fat fromage frais*
100 g/3 1/2 oz	*thick Greek yoghurt*
12.5 cl/4 fl oz	*plain low-fat yoghurt*
4	*mint sprigs, leaves only, chopped*
	white pepper

Grate the courgettes into a bowl, sprinkle them with the salt and set them aside for 30 minutes.

Meanwhile, make the pasta dough. Put the flour into a bowl and make a well in the centre. Add the egg, egg white and oil, and stir them with a fork or wooden spoon, gradually mixing in the flour. Transfer the dough to a lightly floured surface and knead it for a few minutes. The dough should come cleanly away from the surface; if it is too wet, add flour by the tablespoon until the dough is no longer sticky. If the dough is too dry and crumbly to work with, add water by the teaspoon until it is pliable. Continue kneading the dough until it is smooth and elastic—about 10 minutes. (Alternatively, place the dough ingredients in a food processor and process for about 30 seconds.) Wrap the dough in greaseproof paper or plastic film and let it rest for 15 minutes before rolling it out.

To prepare the filling, break up the ricotta with a fork in a large bowl and season it with some black pepper. Squeeze the courgettes dry, a quarter at a time, in a double layer of muslin or a clean tea towel, and add them to the ricotta. Mix well together and set aside.

Divide the dough into three equal portions. Cover two with plastic film or an inverted bowl to keep them from drying out. Using a rolling pin, roll out the third on a floured surface into a sheet about 1 mm (1/16 inch) thick. With a 6 cm (2 1/2 inch) round cutter, cut out 24 circles from the pasta and form them into tortellini, as demonstrated below, using 1 teaspoon of filling for each circle. Repeat the procedure with the remaining pieces of dough and filling to make about 72 tortellini. Set them aside.

To make the sauce, place all the ingredients in a food processor or blender, and blend them until smooth. Transfer the sauce to a small saucepan and warm over very gentle heat while you cook the pasta. Do not allow the sauce to boil.

Add the tortellini to 3 litres (5 pints) of boiling water with 1 1/2 teaspoons of salt. Start testing the tortellini 1 minute after the water returns to the boil, and cook them until they are *al dente*. Drain the pasta and serve it immediately, with the mint-yoghurt sauce and a little chopped mint sprinkled over the top.

EDITOR'S NOTE: Instead of kneading and rolling out the pasta by hand, you can use a pasta machine.

Scorzonera and Asparagus Muffins

Serves 4

Working (and total) time about 30 minutes

Calories 240, Protein 20g, Cholesterol 20mg, Total fat 7g, Saturated fat 4g, Sodium 520mg

4	scorzonera (about 250 g/8 oz), topped, tailed and scrubbed well
12	asparagus spears, trimmed and peeled
4	wholemeal muffins, halved horizontally
4 tsp	low-fat fromage frais
	freshly ground black pepper
1 tbsp	finely chopped mixed fresh herbs (tarragon, chervil, dill, parsley)
125 g/4 oz	low-fat mozzarella cheese, thinly sliced
1 tsp	paprika
2 tsp	finely cut chives

Cook the scorzonera in a saucepan of lightly boiling water, covered, for 10 to 15 minutes, until it is tender when pierced with a sharp knife. Drain the scorzonera and, using the back of a knife, scrape each root gently under cold running water until all the black skin has been removed. Cut each scorzonera root into three pieces of equal length.

Meanwhile, steam the asparagus in a steamer basket over a pan of gently simmering water for about 10 minutes, until it is tender but still crisp. Remove the asparagus from the steamer and place the spears on paper towels to dry.

Preheat the grill to medium. Toast the muffins on their uncut side only. Spread the untoasted side of the warm muffins with the *fromage frais*, and season them with some black pepper and the chopped mixed fresh herbs. Put three asparagus spears on each of four of the halves, and three pieces of scorzonera on each of the other four halves. Lay the mozzarella slices on top of the vegetables. Place the muffins under the grill until the mozzarella has melted and is beginning to bubble and brown slightly—3 to 5 minutes. Garnish the scorzonera muffins with the paprika and the asparagus muffins with the chives. Serve at once.

EDITOR'S NOTE: Scorzonera is similar to the lighter-skinned salsify, which may be used instead in this recipe.

Smoked Cheese Gougère with a Lemon and Fennel Filling

Serves 6

Working time: about 40 minutes

Total time: about 1 hour and 15 minutes

Calories 240, Protein 7g, Cholesterol 80mg, Total fat 15g, Saturated fat 5g, Sodium 260mg

3	*fennel bulbs (about 600g/1¼ lb), cleaned and quartered lengthwise*
2	*lemon balm sprigs (optional)*
1	*stick celery, trimmed and roughly chopped*
⅛ tsp	*salt*
	freshly ground black pepper
1	*lemon, grated rind and juice*
1½ tbsp	*cornflour*
30 g/1 oz	*shelled walnuts, roughly chopped*
	finely chopped fennel leaves, for garnish
	Choux dough
125 g/4 oz	*plain flour*
⅛ tsp	*salt*
⅛ tsp	*cayenne pepper*
75 g/2½ oz	*polyunsaturated margarine*
2	*eggs*
1	*egg white*
30 g/1 oz	*smoked cheese, grated*

Preheat the oven to 220°C (425°F or Mark 7).

First make the choux dough for the gougère. Sift the flour, salt and cayenne pepper on to a sheet of greaseproof paper. Put the margarine and ¼ litre (8 fl oz) of water into a heavy-bottomed saucepan and heat them gently until the margarine melts. Increase the heat to medium high and bring the water and margarine to the boil. Remove the pan from the heat and slide all the dry ingredients off the paper into the liquid, beating vigorously with a wooden spoon. Return the saucepan to the heat and continue to beat the mixture until it forms a ball in the centre of the pan. Remove the pan from the heat and allow the mixture to cool for a few minutes.

Lightly beat the eggs and egg white together. Using an electric hand-held mixer, or beating vigorously with a wooden spoon, gradually incorporate the eggs, a little at a time, into the cooled mixture, beating well after each addition. Beat in the cheese and continue to beat until the mixture forms a smooth, shiny paste. Pipe or spoon the choux dough round the edge of a greased 28 cm (11 inch) ovenproof flan dish, making small mounds of dough that just touch one another.

Bake the gougère in the oven for 10 minutes. Reduce the oven temperature to 190°C (375°F or Mark 5) and continue baking for another 35 to 40 minutes, until the gougère is golden-brown and well risen.

Meanwhile, prepare the filling. Bring 60 cl (1 pint) of water to the boil in a heavy-bottomed saucepan. Add the fennel, lemon balm, if you are using it, celery, salt and some black pepper to the pan. Reduce the heat and simmer the fennel for 5 minutes, or until it is tender but still crisp. Drain the contents of the pan, reserving the liquid; keep the fennel and celery warm until required. Discard the lemon balm. Return the liquid to the pan and add the lemon rind and juice. Bring the liquid to the boil and boil it rapidly until it has reduced to half its original quantity.

In a small bowl, blend the cornflour with 3 tablespoons of water, to form a smooth paste. Add the paste to the lemon-flavoured stock and cook it for a further 2 minutes, stirring frequently, until the sauce thickens. Remove the pan from the heat.

Place the fennel and celery in the centre of the gougère and pour the lemon sauce over the top. Sprinkle the walnuts over the gougère and garnish it with a few finely chopped fennel leaves.

Warm Camembert and Fruit Salad

Serves 4

Working (and total) time: about 20 minutes

Calories 150, Protein 5g, Cholesterol 10mg, Total fat 12g,
Saturated fat 1g, Sodium 380mg

60 g/2 oz	*Camembert, rind removed, cut into 12 cubes*
1 tsp	*crushed mixed white, black, green and pink peppercorns*
100 g/3¹/₂ oz	*broccoli; cut into tiny florets, stalks peeled and finely sliced*
¹/₂ tbsp	*sesame oil*
¹/₂ tbsp	*safflower oil*
1	*garlic clove, lightly crushed*
2.5 cm/1 inch	*piece fresh ginger root, sliced*
1	*large ripe peach, peeled, halved, stoned and sliced, slices halved if too large*
¹/₂	*avocado (about 75 g/2 ¹/₂ oz), peeled and stoned, flesh cut into cubes*
1 tbsp	*balsamic vinegar, or 2 ¹/₂ tsp red wine vinegar mlxed with ¹/₄ tsp clear honey*
¹/₂ tsp	*salt*
60 g/2 oz	*radicchio leaves, washed and dried, torn into pieces*
100 g/3¹/₂ oz	*mixed lettuce leaves, washed and dried*

Roll the cubes of Camembert in the peppercorns and chill them in the refrigerator while preparing the salad.

Place the broccoli in a bowl with 2 tablespoons of cold water, cover with plastic film, leaving a corner open, and microwave on high for 1¹/₂ to 2 minutes, until no longer tough but still very firm. Drain the broccoli, return it to the bowl, cover it and set it aside.

Put the oils in a dish with the garlic and ginger, and cook on medium for 2 to 3 minutes until hot, stirring once or twice during this time. Remove the garlic and ginger with a slotted spoon and discard them. Place the peach slices in the dish with the flavoured oil. Cover the dish as before and microwave on high for 1 minute. Stir the peach slices, add the avocado, cover again and cook on high for another minute. Then add the vinegar, salt and broccoli. Cover and cook on high for a further minute. Finally, toss the radicchio in the dish, stir well, cover the dish and set it aside.

Arrange the mixed lettuce leaves round the edge of a large serving platter, or on four individual plates. Place the Camembert cubes, evenly spaced, on a plate and microwave them on medium for 20 seconds, until just warm. Quickly arrange the warm salad in the centre of the lettuce and sprinkle the Camembert cubes on top. Serve at once.

EDITOR'S NOTE: A nectarine may be substituted for the peach; there is no need to peel a nectarine before use.

Beef and Apple Salad with Stilton Cheese Dressing

Serves 4 as a main course
Working time: about 40 minutes
Total time: about 1 hour and 20 minutes
Calories 340, Protein 28g, Cholesterol 90mg, Total fat
16g, Saturated fat 6g, Sodium 515mg

400 g/14 oz	*thick piece of beef rump or sirloin steak*
1 tbsp	*cracked black peppercorns*
12 5cl/4 fl oz	*stout or dark beer*
4 tbsp	*grated fresh horseradish, or 2 tbsp prepared horseradish, drained*
100 g/3½ oz	*shallot, finely chopped*
120 g/4 oz	*celery, chopped*
2	*tart green apples, peeled, cored and cut into small pieces*
2 tbsp	*cut fresh chives*
1	*bunch watercress, washed and dried*
3½ tbsp	*mayonnaise*
60 g/2 oz	*Stilton cheese, crumbled*
1	*lemon, juice only*
¼ tsp	*salt*

Preheat the oven to 230°C (450°F or Mark 8). Rub the beef with the cracked pepper, pressing the grains into the meat with the palm of your hand. Heat a shallow fireproof casserole over medium-high heat. Set the beef in the pan with its fat side down; briefly sear the beef to render some of the fat. When a thin layer of fat covers the bottom of the pan, turn the beef over and brown it on the other side. Continue turning the beef until it is browned all over— about 5 minutes.

Transfer the casserole to the oven and roast the beef for 10 minutes. Remove the casserole and pour 4 tablespoons of the stout or beer over the roast. Return the roast to the oven and cook it until it is medium rare—about 20 minutes more. Remove the roast from the casserole and set it aside to cool.

Pour the remaining stout or beer into the casserole and set it over medium-high heat. Simmer the liquid, scraping the bottom of the pan with a wooden spoon until any caramelized juices have dissolved—about 2 minutes. Pour the liquid into a small heatproof bowl; set the bowl in the freezer for about 30 minutes.

While the liquid is chilling, assemble the rest of the salad. Trim the roast of fat and cut the beef into julienne. Transfer the beef to a large bowl and add the horseradish, shallot, celery, apples and chives. Pluck the leaves from half of the watercress stems and add the leaves to the mixture.

To make the dressing, lift the layer of congealed fat from the surface of the chilled liquid. Whisk the liquid with the mayonnaise, cheese, lemon juice and salt. Pour the dressing over the contents of the bowl and toss the salad well. Present the salad on a serving platter, garnished with the remaining watercress.

Chicken and Avocado Salad
with Ricotta and Chives

Serves 4 as a main course
Working time: about 20 minutes
Total time: about 50 minutes
Calories 315, Protein 40g, Cholesterol 100 mg,
Total fat 17g, Saturated fat 4g, Sodium 265mg

1 tsp	*safflower oil*
4	*chicken breasts, skinned and boned (500g/ 1 lb)*
1/4 tsp	*salt*
	freshly ground black pepper
250 g/8 oz	*low-fat ricotta cheese*
1 tbsp	*low-fat plain yoghurt*
2 tbsp	*chopped chives*
1	*spring onion, very finely sliced*
1	*head of radicchio or red-leaf lettuce washed and dried*
1	*ripe avocado, stone removed, peeled, fifth rubbed with 1 tbsp fresh lemon juice*
1	*tomato, seeded and finely chopped (optional)*
6	*fresh basil leaves, thinly sliced (optional)*

Heat the safflower oil in a large, heavy frying pan over very low heat. Sprinkle the chicken breasts with 1/8 teaspoon of the salt and some freshly ground pepper, and place them in the pan. Set a heavy plate on top of the chicken breasts to weight them down so that they will cook evenly. Cook the breasts on one side for 5 minutes; turn them over, again cover them with the plate, and cook them for 3 to 4 minutes more. The meat should feel firm but springy to the touch, with no traces of pink along the edges. Transfer the chicken breasts to a plate and refrigerate them while you prepare the rest of the salad.

Put the ricotta, yoghurt, chopped chives and sliced spring onion into a bowl. Mix them well together, then cover the bowl and leave it to stand in a cool place for about 30 minutes.

Arrange a few radicchio or lettuce leaves on four plates. Slice the cooked chicken breasts diagonally and fan out each one of the leaves. Cut the peeled avocado into thin slices and tuck the slices between the chicken slices, then spoon a neat mound of the ricotta mixture on to the base of each chicken fan. If using, sprinkle the chopped tomato and basil over the top and, if you like, a little freshly ground pepper.

EDITOR'S NOTE: Because avocado darkens when exposed to air, it should be rubbed generously with lemon juice immediately after peeling.

42

Veal Fillets with Gorgonzola and Fennel

Serves 4

Working (and total) time: about 40 minutes

Calories 240, Protein 27g, Cholesterol 105mg, Total fat 12g, Saturated fat 2g, Sodium 380mg

500 g/1 lb	veal fillet, trimmed of fat, cut diagonally into 5 mm (¼ inch) thick slices and slightly flattened
1 tbsp	virgin olive oil
2 tbsp	Pernod or unsalted stock
250 g/8 oz	bulb fennel, cut into slices, feathery tops reserved
90 g/3 oz	Gorgonzola cheese, mashed
2 tbsp	skimmed milk chopped
2 tsp	fresh sage, or ½ tsp dried sage
2 tsp	chopped fresh thyme, or ½ tsp dried thyme
⅛ tsp	salt
	freshly ground black pepper

Preheat the oven to 140°C (275°F or Mark 1). Heat the oil in a non-stick frying pan over medium-high heat, add as many pieces of veal as the pan will comfortably hold and cook for 3 to 5 minutes until just tender, turning once and pressing the pieces of veal firmly with a palette knife or spatula to keep them as flat as possible. Transfer the veal to a platter, cover and keep hot in the oven. Cook the remainder of the veal in the same way.

Add the Pernod or stock to the cooking juices in the pan, increase the heat and stir briskly to deglaze. Add the fennel and toss over high heat for 2 to 3 minutes, then remove with a slotted spoon and keep hot with the veal.

Reduce the heat, add the Gorgonzola and milk, and cook gently, stirring, until the cheese has melted and formed a sauce with the cooking juices and milk. Add the chopped sage, thyme, salt and some pepper, and remove the pan from the heat.

To assemble the dish, arrange the meat and fennel on individual plates. Spoon the sauce over the meat and garnish with the reserved fennel tops. Serve immediately.

EDITOR'S NOTE: Adding pernod to the cooking juices heightens the anise flavour of the fennel.

Loin Chop and Artichoke Gratin

Serves 8

Working time: about 25 minutes

Total time: about 50 minutes

Calories 225, Protein 23g, Cholesterol 75mg, Total fat 14g, Saturated fat 6g, Sodium 205mg

8	*loin chops (about 100 g/5 oz each), trimmed of fat*
12	*garlic cloves, peeled*
1 tbsp	*virgin olive oil*
1 tsp	*fresh thyme, or ¹/₂ tsp dried thyme*
¹/₂ tsp	*salt*
	freshly ground black pepper
3	*large globe artichokes*
¹/₂ tsp	*lemon*
30 g/1 oz	*Parmesan cheese, grated*
15 g/¹/₂ oz	*fresh white breadcrumbs*
1 tbsp	*chopped fresh parsley*

Preheat the oven to 200°C (400°F or Mark 6).

Arrange the chops in the base of a shallow ovenproof dish, interspersing them with the garlic cloves. Brush the chops with the oil, sprinkle them with the thyme and season with the salt and some black pepper. Cook, uncovered, in the oven for 15 minutes.

Meanwhile, prepare the artichokes. Bring a saucepan of water to the boil. Break off the stalks from the artichokes and remove the bottom three to four rows of tough outer leaves. Trim off the dark green base of each artichoke using a paring knife. Cut the top 4 cm (1¹/₂ inches) off each artichoke and discard, then pull out the densely packed central leaves to expose the hairy choke. Scoop out the chokes with a teaspoon. While working on the artichokes, rub them frequently with the cut surface of the half lemon to prevent them from discolouring.

Squeeze the juice remaining in the lemon half into the boiling water. Add the artichokes and cook them until tender—about 5 minutes. Drain them well and cut them into eighths or slices.

Remove the chops from the oven, and increase the temperature to 220°C (425°F or Mark 7). Skim off any fat from the juices in the cooking dish. Distribute the artichokes evenly over and around the chops. Combine the Parmesan and the breadcrumbs, then sprinkle this mixture over the chops and artichokes. Return the dish to the oven until the chops are well cooked and the topping is golden-brown—20 to 25 minutes. Sprinkle with the parsley and serve.

Cannelloni Stuffed with Pork and Ricotta

Serves 4

Working (and total) time: about 1 hour

Calories 460, Protein 28g, Cholesterol 45mg,
Total fat 20g, Saturated fat 6g, Sodium 145mg

250 g/8 oz	pork fillet, trimmed of fat and minced
60 g/2 oz	sun-dried tomatoes
90 g/3 oz	low-fat ricotta
30 g/1 oz	fresh basil, finely chopped
	freshly ground black pepper
8	cannelloni tubes
90 cl/1½ pints	unsalted vegetable or chicken stock

Pesto sauce

90 g/3 oz	fresh basil
30 g/1 oz	pine-nuts
3 tbsp	virgin olive oil
1	garlic clove
30 g/1 oz	freshly grated Parmesan cheese

Cut one of the sun-dried tomatoes into strips and re-serve for a garnish. Chop the remaining tomatoes finely and mix them well with the pork, ricotta, basil and a little black pepper. Using your fingers, fill the cannelloni with this stuffing mixture.

To make the pesto, put the basil, pine-nuts, oil and garlic in a food processor or blender, and blend for 2 minutes. Add the Parmesan and blend again briefly.

Bring the stock to a simmer in a pan large enough to take the cannelloni in one layer. Using a slotted spoon, carefully put the cannelloni into the stock, and poach for 15 minutes, or until the pasta is soft and the stuffing feels firm. Drain, reserving the stock, and keep warm.

For the sauce, blend 4 tablespoons of the stock with 2 tablespoons of the pesto, and heat if necessary. Keep any remaining pesto for another use. Arrange the cannelloni on a warmed serving dish, pour a thick ribbon of pesto sauce over them and garnish with the reserved tomato strips.

EDITOR'S NOTE: The cannelloni tubes used in this recipe do not require precooking before they are filled.

Scandinavian Gratin

Serves 6
Working time: about 30 minutes
Total time: about 2 hours
Calories 290, Protein 20g, Cholesterol 85mg,
Total fat 13g, Saturated fat 4g, Sodium 365mg

250 g/8 oz	*pork fillet or loin, trimmed of fat and cut into thin slices*
500 g/1 lb	*potatoes, thinly sliced*
250 g/8 oz	*onions, thinly sliced*
350 g/12 oz	*fresh herring fillets*
1 tsp	*salt*
	white pepper
15 cl/¼ pint	*skimmed milk*
1	*egg yolk*
125 g/4 oz	*smetana*
2	*parsley sprigs, finely chopped (optional)*

Preheat the oven to 220°C (425°F or Mark 7).

Lightly grease a 1.5 to 1.75 litre (2½ to 3 pint) ovenproof gratin dish. Layer the sliced potatoes, onions, herring fillets and pork slices in the dish, beginning and ending with a layer of potatoes and seasoning each layer lightly with the salt and some pepper. Pour the skimmed milk into the dish.

Place the dish in the centre of the oven and bake the gratin for 15 minutes, then reduce the heat to 190°C (375°F or Mark 5) and bake for a further hour. Check that all the contents of the dish are tender by inserting a skewer in the centre of the dish—it should meet with no resistance.

Remove the dish from the oven and carefully pour out the thin juices into a bowl. Beat the egg yolk with the smetana, then beat a couple of spoonfuls of the hot cooking juices into the egg liaison. Whisk this liaison into the remaining juices in the bowl and return the liquid to the dish.

Return to the oven for a further 15 minutes.If the top layer of potatoes is already browned, cover the dish with aluminium foil for the first 10 minutes; if the potatoes still look a little pale at the end of the cooking time, brown briefly under a hot grill.

Cut the gratin into wedges and serve hot, garnished with the chopped parsley, if you are using it.

46

Courgette and Camembert Quiche

Serves 8

Working time: about 30 minutes

Total time: about 1 hour and 35 minutes

Calories 250, Protein 8g, Cholesterol 70mg, Total fat 13g,
Saturated fat 3g, Sodium 3mg

600 g/1¼ lb	*courgettes, sliced*
1 tsp	*polyunsaturated margarine*
1	*onion, finely chopped*
1½ tbsp	*chopped fresh basil, or 1½ tsp dried basil*
140 g/4½ oz	*firm Camembert, rind removed, cut into small pieces*
30 cl/½ pint	*skimmed milk*
2	*eggs, beaten*
⅛ tsp	*salt*
	freshly ground black pepper

Shortcrust pastry

200 g/7 oz	*plain flour*
⅛ tsp	*salt*
90 g/3 oz	*polyunsaturated margarine, chilled*

Preheat the oven to 180°C (350°F or Mark 4). Place the sliced courgettes in a lightly oiled baking dish, cover them with foil and bake them until they are tender—about 20 minutes.

Meanwhile, sift the flour and salt for the pastry into a large bowl, then rub in the chilled margarine with your fingertips until the mixture resembles fine breadcrumbs. Using a round-bladed knife, stir in 3 to 4 tablespoons of cold water to make a firm dough. Turn out the dough on to a lightly floured surface and knead it until it is smooth. Roll out the dough and use it to line a 2.5 cm (1 inch) deep 22 cm (9 inch) flan dish. Prick the base and sides of the pastry case with a fork and chill the case for 20 minutes.

Increase the oven temperature to 200°C (400°F or Mark 6). Bake the pastry case for 15 minutes, then remove it from the oven and set it aside. Reduce the oven temperature to 180°C (350°F or Mark 4).

Melt the margarine in a heavy frying pan and gently fry the onion until it is transparent and tender—5 to 6 minutes. Add the basil and cook for another minute.

Spread half of the onion mixture in the base of the flan case and cover it with half of the courgettes, then add the remaining onion, followed by the rest of the courgettes. Sprinkle the diced cheese on top. In a bowl, whisk together the milk, eggs, salt and some black pepper. Pour this mixture over the layered vegetables. Bake the quiche until it is set and golden brown—30 to 40 minutes. Allow it to cool completely.

Take the quiche to the picnic site in its dish, covered with foil. Cut it into wedges for serving.

Greek-Style Celery and Tomato Salad

Serves 4 as a main course or 6 as a side dish
Working time: about 25 minutes
Total time: about 2 hours (includes cooling)
Calories 150, Protein 6g, Cholesterol 30mg, Total fat 11g,
Saturated fat 4g, Sodium 410mg

500 g/1 lb	ripe tomatoes, quartered, plus six tomatoes, skinned and quartered
1 tbsp	tomato paste
1	large head celery, trimmed, sliced diagonally into 2.5 cm (1 inch) pieces
1 tbsp	virgin olive oil
3 tbsp	fresh lemon juice
2	bay leaves
1/8 tsp	ground coriander
4	spring onions, trimmed and chopped freshly ground black pepper
125 g/4 oz	feta cheese, cut into 1 cm (1/2 inch) cubes
4	black olives, stoned and cut into sixths lengthwise
2 tsp	chopped flat-leaf parsley, plus parsley sprig, for garnish
1 tsp	chopped fresh oregano

Place the unskinned tomato quarters in a bowl with 2 tablespoons of cold water. Cover the bowl with plastic film, pulled back at one edge, and cook the tomatoes on high for 6 minutes, or until they are pulpy; stir them once during this time. Sieve the tomato pulp and stir the tomato paste into it.

Place the celery in a large bowl, and add the sieved tomatoes, garlic, oil, lemon juice, bay leaves and coriander. Stir to mix the ingredients, then cover the bowl as before. Cook on high for 8 minutes, stirring once. Stir in the spring onions and skinned tomato quarters and cook on high for a further 2 minutes, or until the celery is tender but still crisp. Add some black pepper and let the mixture cool—1 1/2 to 2 hours.

Remove the bay leaves and transfer the celery and tomato salad to a rigid plastic container to take to the picnic site. Pack the feta cheese, olive slices and chopped herbs separately.

At the picnic, arrange the salad in a serving dish, and scatter on the cheese, olive slices and chopped herbs. Garnish the salad with the parsley sprig.

Oysters and Pasta Shells in Mornay Sauce

Serves 4

Working (and total) time: about 20 minutes

Calories 335, Protein 21g, Cholesterol 90mg, Total fat 12g, Saturated fat 4g, Sodium 315mg

---

250 g/8 oz	*shucked oysters, drained*
125 g/4 oz	*medium pasta shells*
1 tbsp	*safflower oil*
1 tbsp	*finely chopped shallot*
60 g/2 oz	*Gruyère cheese, coarsely grated*
2 tbsp	*flour*
¹/₄ litre/8 fl oz	*semi-skimmed milk*
	grated nutmeg
¹/₈ tsp	*salt*
	white pepper
1 tbsp	*fresh breadcrumbs*
¹/₂ tsp	*paprika*

Cook the pasta in 1 litre (1³/₄ pints) of boiling water with ¹/₄ teaspoon of salt; start testing the shells after

10 minutes and cook them until they are *al dente*. Drain, put them in a bowl and cover them with cold water.

Place the oil and shallot in another bowl, cover with plastic film or a lid, and microwave it on high for 45 seconds. Toss the cheese with the flour, evenly coating the cheese, and add this mixture to the bowl. Stir in the milk, a pinch of nutmeg, the salt and some white pepper. Cover the bowl again, leaving a slight gap to allow steam to escape, and microwave it on high for 3 minutes. Remove from the oven and stir the sauce.

Drain the reserved pasta and combine it with the sauce. Gently stir in the oysters, then transfer the mixture to a shallow baking dish. Cover the dish and microwave it on medium (50 per cent power) for 5 minutes. Remove the dish from the oven and stir to blend the oyster liquid into the sauce. Combine the breadcrumbs with the paprika and sprinkle them over the top. Serve immediately.

Potatoes Layered with Gruyère and Onions

Serves 6 as a main course
Working time: about 35 minutes
Total time: about 2 hours
Calories 250, Protein 9g, Cholesterol 25mg, Total fat 9g,
Saturated fat 4g, Sodium 210mg

1 kg/2¹/₂ lb	*large potatoes, scrubbed*
1 tbsp	*virgin olive oil*
125 g/4 oz	*spring onions, trimmed and thinly sliced*
1	*garlic clove, crushed*
1	*large sweet red pepper, seeded, deribbed and thinly sliced*
¹/₂ tsp	*salt*
	freshly ground black pepper
125 g/4 oz	*Gruyère cheese, coarsely grated*
6 tbsp	*unsalted chicken stock*
1 tbsp	*chopped parsley*

Put the potatoes into a large saucepan and cover them with cold water. Put on the lid and bring the water to the boil, then reduce the heat and simmer the potatoes for 25 to 30 minutes, until they are almost, but not quite, tender.

Meanwhile, heat the oil in a heavy frying pan over medium heat. Add the spring onions and garlic, and cook them gently until soft but not browned—2 to 3 minutes. Using a slotted spoon, remove the onions and garlic from the pan and set them aside. Add the sweet red pepper slices to the oil remaining in the frying pan. Cover the pan and sweat the pepper slices over low heat for 15 to 20 minutes, until they are soft. Remove the pan from the heat.

Preheat the oven to 220°C (425°F or Mark 7). Grease a 25 by 11 by 7.5 cm (10 by 4¹/₂ by 3 inch) loaf tin. Line the base with non-stick parchment paper.

Drain the potatoes and, holding each one in turn in a clean tea towel, carefully peel off the skins while the potatoes are still hot. Allow the peeled potatoes to cool for 15 to 20 minutes, then cut them into slices a little less than 5 mm (¹/₄ inch) thick.

Arrange the best and largest potato slices in two neatly overlapping rows in the bottom of the loaf tin. Season them with a little of the salt and some black pepper. Cover the potato slices with half of the onions and garlic, and scatter on a quarter of the grated cheese. Sprinkle 1¹/₂ tablespoons of the chicken stock over the top. Add another layer of potato slices, season them with a little more of the salt and some black pepper, and cover them with the red pepper slices. Sprinkle on another quarter of the cheese and 1¹/₂ tablespoons of the stock. Arrange another layer of potato slices in the tin, season them as before, and add the remaining onions and garlic, another quarter of the cheese and 1¹/₂ tablespoons of the stock. Finally, layer the remaining potato slices in the tin, add the remaining salt and a little more black pepper, and sprinkle on the remaining cheese and stock.

Bake the vegetables for 30 to 40 minutes, until the topmost potatoes are golden-brown and all the potatoes are cooked through. Remove the tin from the oven and allow it to stand for 5 minutes. Loosen the sides with a palette knife, then turn the vegetables out on to a flat serving platter. Peel off the lining paper, scatter the chopped parsley over the dish and serve it hot, cut into slices.

Strawberry Cheese Loaf

Serves 10

Working time: about 30 minutes

Total time: about 8 hours and 30 minutes (includes chilling)

Calories 130, Protein 12g, Cholesterol 10mg, Total fat 2g, Saturated fat 1g, Sodium 240mg

500 g/1 lb	low-fat cottage cheese
200 g/7 oz	quark
1 tsp	pure vanilla extract
45 g/1½ oz	caster sugar
2 tsp	powdered gelatine
1	egg white
850 g/1¾ lb	fresh strawberries, six reserved for decoration, the remainder hulled
2 tsp	redcurrant jelly

Strawberry-orange sauce

250 g/8 oz	strawberries, hulled
30 g/1 oz	caster sugar
3 tbsp	fresh orange juice
2 tbsp	Cointreau or other orange flavoured liqueur

Press the cottage cheese through a sieve into a mixing bowl. Beat in the quark, vanilla extract and sugar. Dissolve the gelatine in 2 tablespoons of water, then slowly pour it on to the cheese mixture, beating well all the time. Whisk the egg white until it forms soft peaks. Stir 1 tablespoon of the egg white into the cheese mixture, then use a metal spoon to fold in the remaining egg white.

Line an 18 by 10 by 7.5 cm (7 by 4 by 3 inch) loaf tin with a piece of dampened muslin. Spread a third of the cheese mixture in the base of the tin. Halve 13 of the hulled strawberries and arrange six halves, stalk ends down and cut sides against the muslin, along each long edge of the tin. Between these rows of strawberry halves, make a single layer of whole strawberries. Spoon half of the remaining cheese mixture over the strawberries, then lay another seven strawberry halves against the muslin on each long side of the tin—as before, but this time stalk ends up. Pack the remaining whole strawberries over the cheese mixture in an even layer and spread the last of the cheese mixture evenly on the top, pressing it down with the back of the spoon. Chill the terrine overnight, or until the cheese mixture is well set.

To make the sauce, purée the strawberries in a food processor or blender, and press the purée through a sieve into a small pan. Stir in the sugar, orange juice and Cointreau, and cook the sauce over low heat, stirring it gently, until the sugar has dissolved—about 2 minutes. Leave the sauce to cool.

Just before serving the dessert, slice all but a few of the reserved strawberries. Mix the redcurrant jelly with 1 tablespoon of water in a small saucepan over low heat. Unmould the dessert on to a flat serving dish and arrange the sliced strawberries on top. Brush them with the redcurrant glaze and decorate the dish with the remaining whole strawberries. Serve the terrine cut into slices, accompanied by the sauce.

EDITOR'S NOTE: Once it has reached room temperature, this terrine becomes soft and difficult to slice. If you wish, return it to the refrigerator to firm it up once more before serving or, alternatively, spoon it into portions.

Buckwheat Blinis Topped with Goat Cheese

Makes about 60 blinis
Working time: about 45 minutes
Total time: about 2 hours and 30 minutes (Includes proving)
Per blini: Calories 35, Protein 2g, Cholesterol 10mg, Total fat 2g, Saturated fat trace, Sodium 65mg

35 cl/12 fl oz	skimmed milk
15 g/¹/₂ oz	fresh yeast, or 7 g (¹/₄ oz) dried yeast
125 g/4 oz	buckwheat flour
125 g/4 oz	strong plain flour
¹/₄ tsp	salt
¹/₂ tsp	ground caraway seeds
¹/₂ tsp	crushed black sesame seeds
2 tsp	honey
¹/₂ tbsp	unsalted butter
1	egg, separated

Goat cheese topping

250 g/8 oz	soft goat cheese
1¹/₂ tsp	sesame seeds, toasted
1 tbsp	caraway seeds, toasted
1 tbsp	poppy seeds, toasted
2 tbsp	sunflower seeds, toasted

Warm 2 tablespoons of the milk, blend in the fresh yeast, and leave for about 10 to 15 minutes for the yeast to activate; if using dried yeast, reconstitute according to the manufacturer's instructions.

Sift the flours and salt into a mixing bowl, stir in the caraway and sesame seeds, and make a hollow in the flour mixture. In a small pan, gently warm the remaining milk with the honey and butter until hand hot.

Remove from the heat and stir in the yeast mixture. Pour the milk and yeast mixture, together with the egg yolk, into the flour and blend with a wooden spoon, gradually incorporating the flour until the ingredients are amalgamated. Beat for a further 2 minutes. Leave in a warm place for about 1 hour until well risen and bubbly. The batter should drop easily from a teaspoon; if it is too stiff, beat in a little warm water. Whisk the egg white and fold it into the batter.

Heat a large griddle or non-stick frying pan over medium heat until a few drops of cold water dance when sprinkled on the surface. Drop the batter a teaspoon at a time on to the griddle or frying pan, and use the back of the spoon to spread the batter into rounds about 5 cm (2 inches) in diameter. Cook the blinis until they are covered with bubbles and the undersides are quite dry and golden—1 to 3 minutes. Flip the blinis over and cook them until the second sides are lightly browned—about 1 minute more. Wrap up each batch of blinis in a folded cloth napkin, and keep them warm in a low oven while you cook the remaining batter.

To make the topping, beat the cheese to a smooth, even texture that falls easily from a spoon. To serve, drop a half teaspoon of cheese on each blini, and sprinkle each with one type of seed.

EDITOR'S NOTE: In place of soft goat cheese, you may substitute 125 g (4 oz) hard goat cheese blended with 125 g (4 oz) fromage frais.

To make the dough, sift the flour and ¹/₈ teaspoon of the salt into a bowl, then rub in the margarine until the mixture resembles fine breadcrumbs. Add the egg white and mix, with a round-bladed knife, to form a dough. Knead the dough on a lightly floured surface until smooth.

Roll out the dough thinly then, using a 10 cm (4 inch) plain round cutter, cut out rounds. Fit the rounds into 7 cm (2³/₄ inch) fluted tartlet tins. Trim the edges, then re-knead and re-roll the trimmings. Cut out more rounds and line more tins, continuing until you have lined 18 tins. Place the tins on baking sheets and re-frigerate while you are making the three fillings.

To prepare the spinach filling, heat the oil in a small, heavy frying pan, add the onion and sweet peppers, and cook very gently for 6 to 8 minutes, until soft but not browned. Meanwhile, bring a small saucepan of water to the boil, plunge the spinach leaves into the water and bring back to the boil for 30 seconds. Drain the spinach in a colander, then rinse under cold running water to refresh it. Squeeze the spinach dry and chop finely. Put the spinach and the pepper mixture into a small bowl and set aside.

For the asparagus filling, cut the tips off the asparagus spears and slice the stalks thinly. Cook the asparagus tips and slices in a little boiling water for 2 to 3 minutes, until tender. Drain them in a colander, then refresh under cold running water. Drain well. Cut the cucumber halves in half again lengthwise, then into thin slices. Heat the butter in a small heavy-bottomed saucepan, add the cucumber and cook for 3 to 4 minutes, until softened but not browned. Set the asparagus tips aside, and put the asparagus slices and the cucumber into a small bowl.

To prepare the mackerel filling, remove the skin from the mackerel, then flake the flesh and remove the bones. Put the flesh into a small bowl and set aside.

Preheat the oven to 220°C (425°F or Mark 7). Put the eggs and milk into a bowl, and season with the remaining salt and a little pepper. Whisk lightly together, then stir in the Parmesan cheese. Divide the egg mixture equally among the three bowls of filling and mix each one well.

Fill six of the pastry-lined tins with the asparagus mixture, six with the spinach, and six with the mackerel. Cut the reserved asparagus tips in half and place a piece on each asparagus quiche. Bake the quiches in the oven until they are golden-brown and the filling is set—20 to 25 minutes. Carefully remove the quiches from their tins to a serving plate. Serve warm.

Cocktail Quiches

Makes 18 quiches
Working time: about 1 hour
Total time: about 1 hour and 20 minutes
Per spinach quiche: Calories 140, Protein 5g, Cholesterol 35mg, Total fat 9g, Saturated fat 3g, Sodium 165mg
Per asparagus quiche: Calories 120, Protein 4g, Cholesterol 30mg, Total fat 8g, Saturated fat 2g, Sodium 160mg
Per mackerel quiche: Calories 115, Protein 6g, Cholesterol 35mg, Total fat 7g, Saturated fat 2g, Sodium 230mg

175 g/6 oz	flour
³/₈ tsp	salt
90 g/3 oz	polyunsaturated margarine
1	egg white, lightly beaten
¹/₄ litre/8 fl oz	skimmed milk
	freshly ground black pepper
60 g/2 oz	Parmesan cheese, finely grated

Spinach filling

1 tbsp	virgin olive oil
¹/₂	small onion, finely chopped
¹/₂	small sweet red pepper, chopped
¹/₂	small sweet green pepper, chopped
250 g/8 oz	spinach, stalks removed, washed

Asparagus filling

3	small asparagus spears, trimmed
7 5 cm/3 inch	piece cucumber, peeled, halved lengthwise and seeded
15 g/¹/₂ oz	unsalted butter

Mackerel filling

60 g/2 oz	smoked mackerel fillet

Courgette Soufflés

Makes 40 soufflés
Working time: about 20 minutes
Total time: about 30 minutes

Per souffle: Calories 10, Protein trace, Cholesterol 10mg, Total fat trace, Saturated fat trace, Sodium 20mg

5	courgettes, each about 18 cm (7 inches) long, ends trimmed
1 tsp	polyunsaturated margarine
15 g/¹/₂ oz	plain flour
4 tbsp	skimmed milk
1	egg yolk
30 g/1 oz	mature Cheddar cheese, grated
¹/₄ tsp	Dijon mustard
¹/₄ tsp	salt
	freshly ground black pepper
2	egg whites

Using a canelle knife, cut away thin, evenly spaced strips of skin from the length of each courgette to form a crimped effect. Cut each courgette into eight slices about 2 cm (³/₄ inch) thick. Using a small spoon, scoop out the centre of each slice, taking care not to pierce the base.

Preheat the oven to 220°C (425°F or Mark 7). Cook the courgettes in boiling water until they are bright green and almost tender—about 1 minute. Drain them well in a sieve, and arrange them on a baking sheet lined with non-stick parchment paper.

To prepare the soufflé filling, place the margarine, flour and milk in a small heavy-bottomed saucepan, and whisk until the ingredients are well blended. Place the pan over medium heat and bring to the boil, whisking continuously. Reduce the heat and cook gently for 5 minutes, still whisking continuously. Remove the pan from the heat and whisk in the egg yolk, cheese, mustard, salt and some pepper, until evenly mixed.

In a clean bowl, whisk the egg whites until they are stiff but not dry. Add the egg white to the cheese sauce, one third at a time, carefully folding it into the mixture until all the egg white has been incorporated. Place teaspoons of the soufflé mixture into the courgette containers, filling each to the top.

Bake the soufflés at the top of the oven until the soufflé mixture has risen well and is golden-brown— 5 to 8 minutes. Arrange the courgette soufflés on a serving plate, and serve hot or warm.

EDITOR'S NOTE: Variants of this recipe can be made with artichoke bottoms or hearts, mushrooms or tomato halves in place of the courgette slices.

Miniature Savoury Choux Puffs

Makes about 350 puffs
Working time: about 40 minutes
Total time: about 1 hour
Per 5 puffs: Calories 65, Protein 1g, Cholesterol 25mg,
Total fat 4g, Saturated fat 2g, Sodium 65mg

125 g/4 oz	plain flour
1/4 tsp	salt
2	eggs
1	egg white
90 g/3 oz	polyunsaturated margarine
60 g/2 oz	Parmesan cheese, finely grated
1	garlic clove, crushed
2 tbsp	finely cut fresh chives
1 tbsp	mixed dried herbs

Preheat the oven to 220°C (425°F or Mark 7). Line several baking sheets with non-stick baking parchment. Have ready three piping bags, each fitted with a 1 cm (1/2 inch) plain nozzle. Sift the flour and salt on to a small sheet of greaseproof paper. Lightly beat the eggs and the egg white together.

Put the margarine into a saucepan with 1/4 litre (8 fl oz) of cold water and heat gently until the margarine melts, then bring to the boil. Remove the pan from the heat and tip in the flour, stirring quickly with a wooden spoon at the same time. Return the pan to a moderate heat and stir for a few seconds until the mixture forms a ball. Remove from the heat.

Very gradually add the eggs to the flour and water paste, beating vigorously between each addition with a wooden spoon or a hand-held electric mixer.

Beat the Parmesan and garlic into the choux paste. Put one third of the mixture into a piping bag. Put another third of the mixture into a small bowl and beat in the chives, then spoon into another piping bag. Beat the mixed herbs into the remaining choux paste and spoon into the third piping bag.

Pipe the choux mixtures on to the lined baking sheets in small mounds about 1 cm (1/2 inch) in diameter, spaced apart. Bake in the oven until well risen, golden-brown and crisp—20 to 25 minutes. Remove the puffs from the baking sheets immediately and transfer to wire racks to cool. Serve the puffs within a couple of hours.

EDITOR'S NOTE: The piped dough may be stored for up to 2 hours in the refrigerator before baking. Alternatively, pipe the choux on to foil-lined trays and freeze. Then lift off each foil stack, wrap and store in the freezer. When required, place each foil sheet on a baking sheet and bake.

Party Pinwheels

Makes 240 pinwheels
Working time: about 1 hour and 40 minutes
Total time about 4 hours (includes chilling)
Per prawn pinwheel: Calories 50, Protein 4g, Cholesterol
25mg, Total fat 1g, Saturated fat trace, Sodium 115mg
Per watercress pinwheel: Calories 65, Protein 3g, Cholesterol
trace, Total fat 4g, Saturated fat 1g, Sodium 155mg
Per mushroom pinwheel: Calories 60, Protein 2g, Cholesterol
trace, Total fat 3g, Saturated fat 1g, Sodium 75mg

1	small day-old white tin loaf
1	small day old wholemeal tin loaf
1	small day-old black rye tin loaf

Prawn filling

350 g/12 oz	cooked shelled prawns
1 tbsp	creamed horse radish
1/4 tsp	white pepper
1 tbsp	tomato paste
1 tsp	grated lemon rind
2 tbsp	soured cream or fromage frais

Watercress filling

250 g/8 oz	watercress, washed, thick stems trimmed
250 g/8 oz	medium-fat curd cheese
1/4 tsp	grated nutmeg
1/4 tsp	salt
	freshly ground green peppercorns (optional)

Mushroom filling

350 g/12 oz	button mushrooms, wiped clean and finely chopped
1 tbsp	Madeira or cognac
1 tbsp	Dijon mustard
1/4 tsp	salt
175 g/6 oz	medium-fat curd cheese
1/2 tsp	ground coriander

To make the prawn filling, blend all the ingredients in a food processor to produce a dense but very smooth purée. Chill while you make the other fillings.

To make the watercress filling, plunge the watercress into lightly boiling water for a few seconds, until bright green and slightly limp. Rinse immediately under cold running water, drain and squeeze hard. In a food processor, blend the watercress together with the curd cheese, nutmeg, salt and some freshly ground green pepper, if using, to form a speckled green purée. Chill the purée in the refrigerator.

To make the mushroom filling, put the mushrooms in a sauté pan with the Madeira or cognac, the mustard and salt. Cover the pan and cook over low heat until the mushrooms are cooked through—about 10 minutes. Remove the lid and continue to cook the mushrooms to evaporate any excess liquid, then cool the mixture. Place the cooked mushrooms in a food processor with the curd cheese and coriander, and process to form a smooth, light brown purée. Chill the purée for about 30 minutes.

Meanwhile, slice each loaf horizontally to give eight slices about 1 cm (1/2 inch) thick. Trim off the crusts and flatten each slice with a rolling pin to make it more flexible. Cover the bread with plastic film or a clean, damp cloth until you are ready to use it.

Spread one eighth of the prawn mixture on each slice of white bread, one eighth of the watercress puree on each slice of wholemeal bread and one eighth of the mushroom mixture on each slice of rye bread. Make sure that the filling extends to the edges of the bread. Roll up each slice, starting with a shorter side, to make a tight roll, but taking care not to press out any filling. Wrap the rolls in plastic film and chill them for about 2 hours in the refrigerator.

Unwrap the rolls and use a sharp, serrated knife to slice each one into 10 to 12 thin slices; you may need to discard the first and last slices if ragged. Arrange the pinwheels decoratively on a plate to serve.

Spinach and Ricotta Calzone

Makes 30 calzone

Working time: about 40 minutes

Total time: about 1 hour and 30 minutes

Per calzone: Calories 85, Protein 4g, Cholesterol 10mg,
Total fat 2g, Saturated fat 1g, Sodium 150mg

2 tsp	*sugar*
30 g/1 oz	*fresh yeast, or 15 g (¹/2 oz) dried yeast*
500 g/1 lb	*strong plain flour*
1 tsp	*salt*
1 tbsp	*virgin olive oil*
1	*egg yolk beaten with 2 tsp water*
	Spinach and ricotta filling
500 g/1 lb	*spinach, washed, stems removed*
125 g/4 oz	*low-fat ricotta cheese*
¹/2 tsp	*grated nutmeg*
1 tsp	*pesto*
¹/4 tsp	*salt*
	freshly ground black pepper
125 g/4 oz	*low-fat mozzarella, finely cubed*

To make the dough for the calzone, first stir the sugar into 30 cl (¹/2 pint) of tepid water, then blend in the fresh yeast. Leave to activate until the mixture is frothy—10 to 15 minutes. If you are using dried yeast, reconstitute according to the manufacturer's instructions. Sift the flour and salt into a large bowl and make a well in the centre. Pour in the yeast liquid and the olive oil and mix, gradually incorporating all the flour into the liquid. Remove the dough from the bowl and knead until it is silky to the touch—about 5 minutes. Add a little more flour if the dough is sticky. Put the dough into a lightly oiled bowl and leave in a warm place until the dough has risen to double its size—about 45 minutes.

While the dough is rising, make the filling. Place the spinach with water still clinging to the leaves in a large saucepan. Cover, and steam the spinach over medium heat until wilted—2 to 3 minutes. Drain and squeeze out all water. Put the spinach into a blender or food processor with the ricotta, nutmeg, pesto, salt and some freshly ground pepper, and blend very briefly. Then stir in the mozzarella cubes.

Preheat the oven to 220°C (425°C or Mark 7).

When the dough has risen, place it on a work surface and knead it slightly to knock it down. Roll out the dough as thinly as possible and cut out 30 circles with a 7.5 cm (3 inch) pastry cutter. Put about a teaspoon of the filling in the centre of each circle, moisten the circumference with a little of the egg yolk and water, then fold over and seal in a semi-circle. Brush the tops of each calzone with the remaining egg yolk and water, then make a small incision in each one.

Bake the calzone until well risen and golden in colour—8 to 10 minutes. Serve warm.

EDITOR'S NOTE: The dough may be prepared in advance and refrigerated for up to 24 hours.

Cherry Cheese Tartlets

Makes 12 tartlets
Working time: about 45 minutes
Total time: about 1 hour and 10 minutes
Per tartlet: Calories 100, Protein 5g, Cholesterol 20mg,
Total fat 3g, Saturated fat 1g, Sodium 110mg

3	*sheets phyllo pastry, each about 45 by 30 cm (18 by 12 inches)*
15 g/¹/₂ oz	*unsalted butter, melted*

Spicy cheese filling

250 g/8 oz	*low-fat soft cheese*
15 cl/¹/₄ pint	*plain low-fat yoghurt*
1	*egg*
1 tbsp	*clear honey*
1 tsp	*pure vanilla extract*
¹/₂ tsp	*ground cinnamon*

Glossy cherry topping

1 tbsp	*cherry jam*
¹/₂ tsp	*cornflour*
350 g/12 oz	*cherries, stoned and halved*

Preheat the oven to 190°C (375°F or Mark 5).

Trim 5 cm (2 inches) off one of the short edges of each sheet of phyllo, then cut each sheet into twelve 10 cm (4 inch) squares. Keep the squares covered by a clean, damp cloth to prevent them from drying out,

removing them as needed. Brush twelve 7.5 cm (3 inch) individual round tins with a little melted butter. Stack three squares of phyllo pastry in each tin, fold the edges over to neaten them, then brush the tops lightly with melted butter. Bake the cases in the oven until crisp and lightly browned—about 3 minutes. Leave them to cool in the tins.

Meanwhile, prepare the cheese filling. Put the cheese, yoghurt, egg, honey, vanilla extract and cinnamon into a mixing bowl. Beat the ingredients together with a wooden spoon until smooth, or blend the mixture in a food processor. Divide the filling among the pastry cases, spreading it evenly with the back of a teaspoon. Return the tartlets to the oven and cook them until the filling has set—8 to 10 minutes. Remove from the oven and cool the tartlets in the tins while you make the cherry topping.

Make a glaze by stirring the cherry jam with 3 tablespoons of water in a small saucepan set over low heat. Blend the cornflour to a smooth paste with 1 tablespoon of water. Add the cornflour paste to the jam solution, bring to the boil and cook, stirring, until the mixture thickens and clears—about 2 minutes. Arrange the cherry halves on top of the cheese mixture and brush with the cherry glaze. Allow to set for a few minutes before unmoulding and serving.

Cheesecake with Strawberries and Kiwi Fruit

Serves 10

Working time: about 40 minutes

Total time: about 3 hours

Calories 175, Protein 9g, Cholesterol 65mg, Total fat 7g, Saturated fat 1g, Sodium 120mg

90 g/3 oz *digestive biscuits, crushed*
125 g/4 oz *low-fat ricotta cheese*
250 g/8 oz *quark*
2 *eggs, whites and yolks separated*
1 tbsp *wholemeal flour*
3 tbsp *clear honey*
2 tsp *fresh orange juice*
15 cl/¼ pint *plain low-fat yoghurt*
60 g/2 oz *sultanas, chopped*
4 *large strawberries, hulled and sliced*
2 *kiwi fruits, peeled and sliced*

Grease an 18 cm (7 inch) flan dish. Line the base with greaseproof paper and grease the paper. Spread the biscuit crumbs on the base and flatten the biscuit layer with the back of a spoon.

Put the ricotta in a bowl with the quark, egg yolks, flour, honey, orange juice and yoghurt and beat with a wooden spoon until the mixture is smooth. Microwave the mixture on medium for 7 to 8 minutes or until thick, whisking it every 2 minutes.

Stir the sultanas into the mixture. Whisk the egg whites until they stand in stiff peaks and fold them into the cheesecake mixture. Spoon the mixture evenly over the biscuit base.

Microwave the cheesecake on medium for 10 to 12 minutes, or until it is just set in the centre, giving the dish a quarter turn every 3 minutes. Leave the cheesecake to stand until cool, then put the dish in the refrigerator for about 2 hours to chill the cake and make it firm enough to unmould.

Run a knife round the cheesecake to loosen it from the sides of the dish. Put a flat plate over the cheesecake and invert plate and dish together. Lift off the dish, remove the paper from the base of the cheesecake and turn it on to a serving dish. Decorate the top with the slices of strawberry and kiwi fruit.

Redcurrant and Blackcurrant Cheesecake

Serves 12
Working time: about 30 minutes
Total time: about 3 hours
Calories 195, Protein 7g, Cholesterol 30mg, Total fat 10g,
Saturated fat 3g, Sodium 180mg

90 g/3 oz *brown flour*
30 g/1 oz *wholemeal semolina*
1 tsp *baking powder*
45 g/1 $\frac{1}{2}$ oz *unsalted butter*
3 tbsp *clear honey*
500 g/1 lb *medium-fat curd cheese*
15 cl/$\frac{1}{4}$ pint *plain low-fat yoghurt*
1 tsp *pure vanilla extract*
1 *egg*
250 g/8 oz *redcurrants, picked over and stemmed*
250 g/8 oz *blackcurrants, picked over and stemmed*
60 g/2 oz *caster sugar*
4 tsp *arrowroot*

Preheat the oven to 180°C (350°F or Mark 4). Grease an 18 cm (7 inch) loose-based square cake tin.

To make the shortcake base, sift the brown flour, semolina and baking powder into a bowl. Rub in the butter with your fingertips untii the mixture resembles breadcrumbs. Using a fork, stir in 1 tablespoon of the honey and 2 teaspoons of cold water. Knead the dough on a lightly floured surface, then roll it out and cut it to fit the cake tin. Lower the dough into the tin and press it well against the base and sides. Prick the dough with a fork and bake it for 10 minutes. Remove it from the oven and reduce the oven temperature to 150°C (300°F or Mark 2).

Meanwhile, beat the curd cheese, yoghurt, remaining honey and vanilla extract in a mixing bowl with a wooden spoon. Add the egg and beat the mixture until smooth Pour the mixture into the cake tin, then bake the cheesecake until the filling has set—about 1 hour. Let it cool in the tin, then transfer it to a plate.

While the cheesecake cooks, put the redcurrants and blackcurrants in separate saucepans and distribute the caster sugar between the two pans. Cook the currants very gently for 2 minutes, shaking the pans occasionally, until the currants are softened but still whole. Strain the juice from the blackcurrants through a nylon sieve. Return the juice to the pan and put the fruit in a bowl. Strain the redcurrant juice through a clean nylon sieve; return the juice to the redcurrant pan and put the redcurrants in a second bowl.

Blend the arrowroot with 2 tablespoons of water, then stir half into each saucepan. Bring both pans of juice to the boil, stirring, and cook for 1 minute. Stir the thickened redcurrant juice gently into the redcurrants and the thickened blackcurrant juice into the blackcurrants. Chill the currants until the cheesecake has cooled. Arrange bands of the redcurrants and blackcurrants on top of the cheesecake.

EDITOR'S NOTE: The blackcurrants can be replaced by blueberries; $\frac{1}{2}$ teaspoon of cinnamon or $\frac{1}{4}$ teaspoon of mace can be added to the dough for the base.

Muesli Cheese Tart

Serves 12

Working time: about 30 minutes

Total time: about 2 hours

Calories 170, Protein 8g, Cholesterol 35mg, Total fat 8g, Saturated 3g, Sodium 80mg

350 g/12 oz	*low-fat soft cheese*
1 tbsp	*clear honey*
1	*egg*
1/2 tsp	*pure vanilla extract*
20 cl/7 fl oz	*plain low-fat yoghurt*
2 tbsp	*toasted and chopped shelled hazelnuts*
1	*lime, rind only, julienned and blanched*

Hazelnut muesli base

3 tbsp	*clear honey*
30 g/1 oz	*unsalted butter*
90 g/3 oz	*rolled oats*
30 g/1 oz	*raisins*
1 tbsp	*toasted and chopped shelled hazelnuts*
1 tbsp	*chopped dried apples*

Preheat the oven to 170°C (325°F or Mark 3). Grease a 35 by 11 cm (14 by 4¹/₂ inch) loose-based plain or fluted oblong tart tin.

To make the muesli base, heat the honey and butter in a saucepan, stirring occasionally. When the butter has melted, remove the pan from the heat and stir in the oats, raisins, hazelnuts and dried apples. Spread the muesli mixture over the base of the tin and level the top with a small palette knife.

Put the soft cheese, honey, egg and vanilla extract in a mixing bowl with all but 3 tablespoons of the yoghurt. Mix the ingredients together with a wooden spoon, then beat them until smooth. Spoon the mixture over the muesli base and level the top with a small palette knife. Bake the cheesecake in the centre of the oven until the filling feels firm when touched in the centre—20 to 25 minutes.

Remove the cake from the oven and spread the remaining yoghurt over the top. Return the cake to the oven for 5 minutes, until the topping has set.

Let the cake cool in the tin. When it reaches room temperature, transfer it to a plate, sprinkle hazelnuts along both sides of the cake and strew the lime julienne down the middle.

EDITOR'S NOTE: To toast hazelnuts, put them on a baking sheet in a preheated 180°C (350°F or Mark 4) oven for 10 minutes.

Cheese Valentine
with Blackberries

Serves 10

Working time: about 20 minutes

Total time: about 6 hours (includes chilling)

Calories 120, Protein 12g, Cholesterol 6mg, Total fat
2g, Saturated fat 1g, Sodium 345mg

750 g/1¹/₂ lb *low-fat cottage cheese*
175 g/6 oz *mild, creamy goat cheese*
4 tbsp *caster sugar*
600 g/1¹/₄ lb *blackberries or strawberries*

Purée the cottage cheese in a food processor or a blender until it is completely smooth. With the motor running, blend in the goat cheese a tablespoon at a time. Stop once or twice during the process to scrape down the sides. Add the sugar and blend it in.

Cut a single thickness of muslin large enough to encase the cheese mixture as it drains. Wet the muslin in cold water, then wring it out. Line a large *coeur à fromage* mould, sieve or colander with the muslin, pressing it in place and smoothing it out with your fingers so that the surface of the finished cheese will be uniformly even.

Spoon the cheese mixture into the lined container. Smooth the top of the cheese mixture and fold the edges of the muslin over it. If you are using a sieve or colander, place it over a deep bowl; if you are using a *coeur à fromage* mould, put it on a plate. Refrigerate the assembly until the whey has thoroughly drained from the cheese—about 6 hours.

To unmould the drained cheese, open the muslin and invert a serving plate over the mould or sieve. Turn both mould and plate over together, then lift away the mould and the muslin.

Serve the valentine chilled. Ring the plate with some of the berries; present the rest in a separate dish.

Raisin Cheesecake

Serves 12

Working time: about 1 hour
Total time: about 5 hours (includes chilling)
Calories 120, Protein 7g, Cholesterol 11mg, Total fat 3g,
Saturated fat 2g, Sodium 150mg

45 g/1¹/₂ oz *sultanas*
45 g/1¹/₂ oz *raisins*
¹/₄ litre/8 fl oz *plain low-fat yoghurt*
90 g/3 oz *low-fat creamy soft cheese*
300 g/10 oz *low-fat cottage cheese*
1 tsp *pure vanilla extract*
100 g/3¹/₂ oz *caster sugar*
12.5 cl/4 fl oz *semi-skimmed milk*
1 tbsp *powdered gelatine*
3 *egg whites, at room temperature*

Put the sultanas and raisins in a small bowl and pour ¹/₄ litre (8 fl oz) of hot water over them. Set the bowl aside.

Purée the yoghurt, soft cheese, cottage cheese, vanilla extract and half the sugar in a food processor or a blender. Scrape the cheese mixture into a large bowl.

Pour the milk into a small saucepan. Sprinkle the gelatine over the milk and let it stand until the gelatine softens—about 5 minutes. Heat the milk over medium heat, stirring until the gelatine is dissolved. Stir the milk into the cheese mixture and set it aside.

Put the egg whites into a deep bowl. Set up an electric mixer; you will need to start beating the egg whites as soon as the syrup is ready.

To prepare Italian meringue, heat the remaining sugar with 2 tablespoons of water in a small saucepan over medium-high heat. Boil the mixture until the bubbles rise to the surface in a random pattern, indicating that the water has nearly evaporated and the sugar is beginning to cook.

With a small spoon, drop a little of the syrup into a bowl filled with iced water. If the syrup dissolves immediately, continue cooking the syrup. When the syrup dropped into the water can be rolled between your fingers into a supple ball, begin beating the egg whites on high speed. Pour the syrup down the side of the bowl in a thin, steady stream. When all the syrup has been incorporated, decrease the speed to medium continue beating until the egg whites are glossy, have formed stiff peaks and have cooled to room temperature—about 10 minutes. Increase the speed to high and beat the meringue for 1 minute more.

Line a 20 cm (8 inch) cake tin with plastic film. Drain the sultanas and raisins and scatter them in the bottom of the tin. Mix about one third of the meringue into the cheese mixture to lighten it. Gently fold in the rest of the meringue, then pour the cheesecake mixture into the lined tin. Chill the cheesecake for 4 hours.

To turn out the cheesecake, invert a serving plate top of the tin then turn both over together. Lift away the tin, peel off the plastic film, and slice the cheesecake for serving.